Electric Cars and the Resource Challenge

This book is the first to fully explore the short- and long-term impact of the global electric car rollout on the supply of raw materials.

The world has gone from zero to almost 1.5 billion fossil fuel cars in circulation today, contributing significantly to the global climate crisis and necessitating a total transition to electric vehicles in the coming decades. This book responds to key questions surrounding the increase of electric car usage, such as will there be sufficient resources available to permanently supply a future world population of ten billion with electric cars? What is the risk that the supply of essential raw materials will be hampered by geopolitical problems, or that mining capacity cannot be quickly scaled up? How does the switch from fossil fuel vehicles to electric cars impact the recycling of scrap cars? It contains detailed information about the material composition of electric and fossil fuel cars in relation to stocks and relative scarcity of corresponding materials in the earth's crust and estimates the ultimate annual consumption of metals based on predicted population growth.

This book is an important tool for decision-makers in national ministries and international bodies, highlighting how to adopt a global long-term raw materials policy to protect the interests of future generations and global fairness. It provides necessary forecasting insight to industry leaders and specialists, policymakers, and researchers.

Theo Henckens, PhD, has been an international advisor to governments and companies with regard to environment and water management. Between 2013 and 2024, Henckens was a research fellow at the Copernicus Institute of Utrecht University, The Netherlands. He has published extensively in the field of scarce raw materials.

Routledge Focus on Environment and Sustainability

The Economics of Estuary Restoration in South Africa
Douglas J. Crookes

Urban Resilience and Climate Change in the MENA Region
Nuha Eltinay and Charles Egbu

Global Forest Visualization
From Green Marbles to Storyworlds
Lynda Olman and Birgit Schneider

Sustainable Marketing and the Circular Economy in Poland
Key Concepts and Strategies
Anita Proszowska, Ewa Prymon-Ryś, Anna Kondak, Aleksandra Wilk and Anna Dubel

Risk Management for Water Professionals
Technical, Psychological and Sociological Underpinnings
Anna Kosovac

Climate Perspectives from the Congo Basin
Bila-Isia Inogwabini

Everyday Agri-Environmental Governance
The Emergence of Sustainability through Assemblage Thinking
Jérémie Forney, Dana Bentia, and Angga Dwiartama

Electric Cars and the Resource Challenge
Theo Henckens

For more information about this series, please visit: www.routledge.com/Routledge-Focus-on-Environment-and-Sustainability/book-series/RFES

Electric Cars and the Resource Challenge

Theo Henckens

First published 2025
by Routledge
4 Park Square, Milton Park, Abingdon, Oxon OX14 4RN

and by Routledge
605 Third Avenue, New York, NY 10158

Routledge is an imprint of the Taylor & Francis Group, an informa business

© 2025 Theo Henckens

The right of Theo Henckens to be identified as author of this work has been asserted in accordance with sections 77 and 78 of the Copyright, Designs and Patents Act 1988.

All rights reserved. No part of this book may be reprinted or reproduced or utilised in any form or by any electronic, mechanical, or other means, now known or hereafter invented, including photocopying and recording, or in any information storage or retrieval system, without permission in writing from the publishers.

Translated and adapted from the Dutch language edition by Theo Henckens, with further language editing by Serena Lyon.
Hoeveel elektrische auto's kan de wereld aan? De grondstoffenuitdaging
by Theo Henckens
Published 2024 by Brave New Books
ISBN: 9789464808599

Trademark notice: Product or corporate names may be trademarks or registered trademarks, and are used only for identification and explanation without intent to infringe.

British Library Cataloguing-in-Publication Data
A catalogue record for this book is available from the British Library

ISBN: 978-1-032-83313-2 (hbk)
ISBN: 978-1-032-83460-3 (pbk)
ISBN: 978-1-003-50943-1 (ebk)

DOI: 10.4324/9781003509431

Typeset in Times New Roman
by Newgen Publishing UK

Contents

Preface *vii*

1 Toward electric driving in a fair world   1
2 Protecting climate may bite resources conservation   16
3 The electric car and the energy transition: conflict or not?   41
4 Sensitivity analysis   53
5 Five critical metals in electric cars   58
    5.1 Copper: aorta of the energy transition 58
    5.2 Lithium lakes 69
    5.3 Cobalt from Congo: a story of winners and losers 76
    5.4 War on the nickel exchange 84
    5.5 Greenland and its rare earths are not for sale 93
6 The circularity of electric cars   103
7 The market in service of fair resource management   126
    Epilogue   145

Index   *147*

Preface

After completing my PhD in 2016, I wanted to write a book to share my knowledge on resource depletion with a wider audience. The publisher Elsevier was interested in the topic, but felt I should focus on a scientific audience. The contact with Elsevier culminated in 2021 in a thick book titled *Governance of the World's Mineral Resources: Beyond the Foreseeable Future*. Although I was pleased with the result, the book was not very accessible and was pricey. I remember discussions with Elsevier about this: I thought a book that cost around €100 would be little read, and I was right.

However, my desire to make my knowledge about our increasingly scarce resources more widely accessible did not diminish. The result is this book, which describes the impact of the rollout of the electric car on the availability of raw materials. Crucial in this context is the perspective of fair distribution: does not every world citizen have an equal right to an electric car? In this book, I explore whether such equity is feasible from a resource and energy availability perspective, or whether fundamental changes are needed to ensure comfortable and sustainable mobility for all.

I limit myself in this book to an exploration of the impact of the electric car on resource availability, although there are also many environmental, political, and social problems associated with resource extraction. For information on the impact of resource extraction on the environment, I refer the reader to the relevant literature.

For their contribution and support in writing this book, I would like to thank the following people. Paul Luttikhuis gave me the idea of describing the problem of resource availability from the perspective of the car. Not only did he inspire me to make my language more accessible, but he also provided some very readable texts, for which I am grateful. I had some interesting discussions with Paul Dietz and Martijn Boelhouwer of Autorecycling Nederland, who also arranged visits for me to a car dismantling company and a post-shredder company. I would also like to thank Peter Driessen of Utrecht University, without whose support it would have been a lot harder to access all the scientific literature that I wished to consult. For her conscientious work, I would like to thank proofreader Serena Lyon. Finally, thanks to my partner Anni Joosten, for her unfailingly loving support.

I dedicate this book to my late wife Nelleke Rögels, to my children Josée and Guy, and especially to my grandchildren Floris, Friso, Jiska, Sigrid, Elof, Reinout, and Quintijn. They will be able to ascertain whether I have worried needlessly, which I sincerely hope.

1 Toward electric driving in a fair world

This book is about raw materials, or, to be more precise, metals. Starting from the idea that every country has the same right to prosperity, I ask the question whether there are enough metals available to continue meeting demand. The question is urgent, because metals are desperately needed for the energy transition, which in turn is needed to end the use of fossil fuels—the main cause of climate change. Renewable energy sources—whether energy generated by wind turbines and solar panels or batteries capable of storing electricity—all require large amounts of metals.

I tell my story based on the automobile—specifically the passenger car. In this story, many facets of the energy transition come together. Just as the energy supply in the second half of this century will be incomparable to that of today, the use of the passenger car may also undergo an unprecedented transformation. Who knows, private car ownership may even start to become a thing of the past again.

> *Gasoline or electricity? The question was already debated in the early days of the automobile. Thomas Edison, the man of electricity, was unsure at first and encouraged car maker Henry Ford to continue his experiments with the gasoline car.*[1] *After all, lead-acid batteries, the only rechargeable kind at Edison's disposal, were far too heavy for an automobile to be able to travel any distance.*
>
> *In 1903, Edison realized that an electric car might be a possibility after all.*[2] *He had invented the nickel-iron battery, which could also be recharged and was much lighter than lead*

DOI: 10.4324/9781003509431-1

batteries. Edison was sure: "Electricity is the thing. [...] There is not that almost terrifying uncertain throb and whirr of the powerful combustion engine. There is no water-circulating system to get out of order—no dangerous and evil-smelling gasoline and no noise."[3] In around 1919, more than one-third of the cars in the United States were electric.

A total of 4,192 passenger cars were produced in the United States in 1900. Of these, 1,681 had steam-powered engines, 1,575 had electric motors, and only 396 had internal combustion engines. The electric car was clearly more popular than the dirty and noisy gasoline car. The steam car had the disadvantage that it used more energy than the electric car and had to carry a lot of water.

Henry Ford wasn't going to let Edison change his mind so easily. He continued to develop his famous Model T, an affordable internal combustion engine car for the American middle class that could be mass-produced, selling over 10,000 of them in 1909 alone. Production of the Model T ended in 1927, immediately after the 15 millionth example rolled off the assembly line.

Nevertheless, his success did not stop Ford from experimenting with an electric-powered car with Edison. In an interview in The New York Times on January 11, 1914, Ford mentions that: "The problem so far has been to build a storage battery of light weight which would operate for long distances without recharging. Mr. Edison has been experimenting with such a battery for some time."[4] Ultimately, the experiment failed and it took nearly a century for the electric car to get another chance. The electric car therefore lost the battle against the gasoline car because of its limited range and the lack of electricity in large parts of the countryside. The gasoline car was simply better suited to the conditions of the time.

In America, the first internal combustion engine car was built in 1893, eight years later than in Germany. In 1908, the Model T cost $850, but by 1924 its price had dropped to $290, although it still had a profit margin of $90, which is more than 30%—something that today's mass producers of cars can only dream of. By 1934, one in five Americans owned a car.[5] This means that, 90 years ago, car ownership in the United States was already as high as today's average car ownership worldwide. Most of

> *these cars were the Model T and its successors: the Model T was the people's car for Americans. In 1934, in impoverished Germany, only one in 75 people owned a car, although the first car with an internal combustion engine was built as early as 1885 by Carl Benz in Mannheim, Germany. This was reason for Hitler to have freeways built and to push the production of the German "volkswagen" (people's car), which was designed by Hitler's friend Ferdinand Porsche in 1935. First produced in 1939 under the name* Kraft durch Freude *(KdF), it was renamed* Volkswagen *(Beetle) after World War II. In 1972, the Beetle supplanted the Model T as the best-selling car of all time; 21 million Beetles were eventually produced. In 1962, one in ten Germans, one in 7.8 French, and one in 8.5 British owned a car. However, Americans were still far ahead, at one in 2.8.*[6]

Much has changed in the century and a half since Carl Benz built the first automobile in Germany. While the first cars looked like carriages with an engine, a design of their own gradually emerged, dictated by the efficiency requirements of the wind tunnel. This was logical, as the pressure to reduce fuel consumption increased. Not only fuel consumption but also the use of raw materials—expressed in grams per driven kilometer—has declined sharply, primarily because cars last much longer than before but also because of the increased use of lighter materials such as plastics and aluminum instead of steel. On the other hand, cars have on average become larger. Nevertheless, no matter how economical and efficient cars become, the continued growth in the number of cars in the world will ultimately mean the end of the fossil-fuel car.

Transport accounts for about a quarter of global CO_2 emissions, almost half of which is from passenger cars. The remainder is from freight traffic (about 30%) and aviation and shipping (both about 10%). See Figure 1.1. Despite catalytic converters in car exhausts, road traffic is still responsible for the largest share of nitrogen oxide (NO_x) emissions. Nitrogen in the form of NO_x should not be confused with nitrogen in the form of ammonia, of which agriculture accounts for a major part. Traffic is also responsible for a substantial share of particulate matter emissions, especially in urban areas. Previously, there was also the emission of hydrocarbons, which led to serious smog

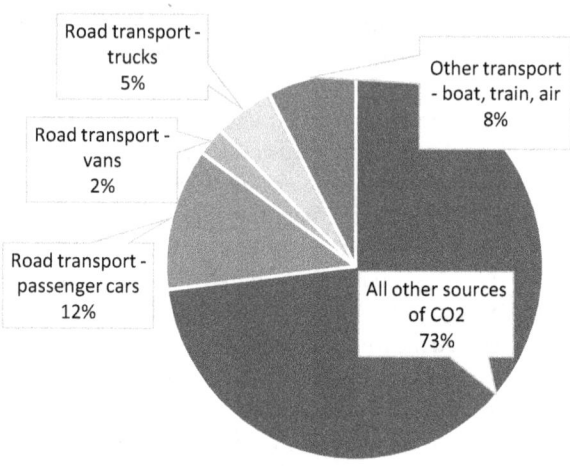

Figure 1.1 Contribution of the transport sector to greenhouse gas emissions in 2017.

Sources: Sims, R., Schaeffer, R., Creutzig, F., Cruz-Núñez, X., D'Agosto, M., Dimitriu, D., Figueroa Meza, M.J., Fulton, L., Kobayashi, S., Lah, O., McKinnon, A., Newman, P., Ouyang, M., Schauer, J.J., Sperling, D., and Tiwari, G. 2014. Transport. In: *Climate Change 2014: Mitigation of Climate Change. Contribution of Working Group III to the Fifth Assessment Report of the Intergovernmental Panel on Climate Change*, Edenhofer, O., Pichs-Madruga, R., Sokona, Y., Farahani, E., Kadner, S., Seyboth, K., Adler, A., Baum, I., Brunner, S., Eickemeier, P., Kriemann, B., Savolainen, J., Schlömer, S., von Stechow, C., Zwickel, T., and Minx, J.C., eds. Cambridge University Press, Cambridge. www.ipcc.ch/site/assets/uploads/2018/02/ipcc_wg3_ar5_chapter8.pdf; "Greenhouse gas emissions from transport in Europe." www.eea.europa.eu/data-and-maps/indicators/transport-emissions-of-greenhouse-gases/transport-emissions-of-greenhouse-gases-7.

problems, and of toxic lead. Emissions of hydrocarbons, nitrogen oxides, and carbon monoxide have been greatly reduced by the mandatory installation of catalytic converters in car exhausts, while almost no leaded gasoline has been sold since the mid-1990s. The reason for this is that lead-based gasoline damages catalytic converters and well-performing substitutes for tetraethyl lead have been developed as anti-knock agents.

In 2015, Volkswagen, the world's largest car company, was found to have developed software to make its diesel vehicles appear cleaner than they are. Volkswagen was not the only company fooling environmental and climate tests with this sham software—Mitsubishi, Daimler,

Jeep, Audi, Suzuki, and others were also named. Unbeknownst to the automotive industry, the scandal heralded the end of the traditional internal combustion engine. "Clean" and "fuel-efficient" have for some time been as important for automobiles as comfort and reliability, and the gasoline engine is facing increasing competition from electrically powered cars.

For a long time, the auto industry—especially in Germany—put off the transition to electric driving. Companies such as BMW and Volkswagen laughed off Tesla, the new kid on the block. But they are laughing no longer, now that the growth of electric cars is unstoppable and the American company has overtaken car giants such as Volkswagen. The Chinese car brand BYD (Build Your Dreams) comes a close second,[7] followed by SAIC (also Chinese), Volkswagen, and Geely (again Chinese, owner of Volvo and Polestar). Meanwhile, German car manufacturers have fully embraced the move to electric driving as their new revenue model. There may be a future in which hydrogen is the main energy carrier, or in which completely different revolutionary technologies are developed, but for now, the automotive industry is concentrating on electric driving.

Pressure is also growing from governments, for example in the European Union and California, to get rid of fossil fuels in order to meet international climate agreements made in Paris in 2015. After constantly tightening the rules for emissions per kilometer, the curtain finally seems to be falling on gasoline and diesel cars as, starting in 2035, many Western countries will ban the sale of new cars with fuel engines.

> *In the European Union's decision to ban fossil-fuel vehicles from 2035, Germany has stipulated that cars will still be allowed to use synthetic, CO_2-neutral fuel. It appears that the specific engine sound of their Porsche or BMW is still sacred for some Germans. Although synthetic fuel may be climate-neutral, particulate matter and nitrogen oxides are still produced in just as large quantities as from fossil fuels. Will the future fossil-fuel cars still running be looked at with the same feeling with which ex-smokers regard cigarettes: with a mixture of physical disgust and the idea that they are antisocial, but also with some nostalgia?*

In the fall of 2022, at the annual auto show in Detroit[8] where Ford, Chrysler, and General Motors showed their latest models, there was, of course, one car that was even faster, more beautiful, and bigger than the other. But most strikingly, almost all of them were electrically powered. As President Joe Biden said during his visit to the auto show: "The great American road trip is going to be fully electrified."

The transition from fossil-fuel to electric cars is not illogical or unexpected. In fact, it is perhaps extraordinary that it has taken so long. In his book, *Clean Disruption of Energy and Transportation,*[9] Tony Seba makes the following nine arguments for the electric car:

1. The electric motor is five times more energy-efficient.
2. The electric vehicle is ten times cheaper to charge.
3. The electric vehicle is ten times cheaper to maintain.
4. The electric vehicle will disrupt the gasoline aftermarket. A pity for the sector, but good for the consumer.
5. The electric vehicle can be charged wirelessly.
6. The electric vehicle has a modular design architecture.
7. Software development in the electric car is far ahead of the one in fossil-fuel cars.
8. Solar and electric vehicles are 400 times more land-efficient.
9. Electric vehicles can contribute to grid storage and other services.

While Seba's numbers may not be exact, they do indicate the direction. However, offset against these advantages of the electric car over the fossil-fuel car is the disadvantage of greater resource consumption per car. The claim that electric cars will make on the world's resources will depend mainly on the future number of cars. In calculating resource consumption, I use the scenario that future car ownership in the world will be the same as in the European Union. After all, every country and every person has the same right to prosperity and therefore to the same level of car ownership as other countries/people. Equal prosperity of countries is therefore my starting point in explorations of the carrying capacity of the Earth. I therefore do not assume that existing inequality, poverty, and deprivation in the world are a given fact in the longer term.

In my exploration of the electric car's use of the world's resource base, I assume that the world's population continues to grow to ten billion people, after which it stabilizes. This number is taken from a United Nations forecast.[10] I call this scenario—with ten billion people with a level of prosperity of that in the European Union in 2050—the fair scenario.

> A scenario is not a prediction. A scenario is meant to show what the consequences will be if the scenario becomes reality. Dennis Meadows, one of the leading authors of the famous book Limits to Growth, published in 1972, emphasized recently that the model that scientists used half a century ago was intended to run through several scenarios and show the effects of each scenario.[11] Scenarios are therefore the answer to "what if?" questions. Without future scenarios, policy development is not possible.

In 2022, over 1.4 billion passenger cars were driving around in the world, equivalent to about 18% of the current world population. That means there are 18 cars for every 100 people. In the European Union, there are about 60 passenger cars for every 100 people, and these cars account for almost 90% of the number of vehicles on the road. The number of trucks, vans, and buses is relatively small compared to the number of passenger cars (about 2%, 10%, and 0.3% of the total number of vehicles, respectively[12]), but, of course, they each use more energy and raw materials.

Because I want to get an idea of the future resource consumption of road transport and because my calculations are exploratory in nature, I assume that all these other vehicles are also passenger cars. In this way, I arrive at a number of almost 1.6 billion vehicles on global roads in 2022, and 68 vehicles for every 100 inhabitants in the European Union. I therefore assume that the number of trucks, vans, and buses increases with the number of passenger cars; that is, for every 88 new passenger cars, there will be ten new vans, two new trucks, and 0.3 new buses. For ease of calculation, I assume that all these vehicles weigh the same as an average passenger car and are composed of the same raw materials. Of course, this is not quite correct, but given the global nature of the calculations, I think I may apply this approximation. After all, the outcome will not be very different from an outcome based on much more precise calculations. I therefore call this whole mixture of vehicles "electric cars." If every 100 people own 68 cars, then ten billion people will own nearly seven billion cars.

To make a rough estimate of future resource use by all these electric cars, I make four assumptions:

Assumption 1: World vehicle production increases at a constant rate of 2.3 million vehicles per year for the time being, until car ownership everywhere in the world equals that of the European Union in 2020, which is 68 vehicles per 100 inhabitants.

I make this assumption because the growth in vehicle production in the world has been roughly linear[i] over the past two decades, from 58 million vehicles per year in 2000, to 98 million per year in 2018.[13] There was a production dip in the financial crisis years of 2008 and 2009, and between 2018 and 2021, mainly because of the coronavirus pandemic. Excluding these temporary production declines, new car production grew by about 2.3 million each year.

Prosperity, expressed in terms of Gross Domestic Product (GDP) per capita, has increased exponentially[ii] since 1980, at an average rate of about 3.5% per year. The fact that the number of vehicles in the world is rising less rapidly than average wealth can be explained by increasing urbanization, resulting in the expansion of public transport, combined with some saturation in car ownership in the most affluent countries. New cars are being added and old cars are being scrapped, and the resulting balance is that the number of vehicles on the world's roads increased by an average of about 45 million each year between 2005 and 2020.[14] This corresponds to an average vehicle life of about 20 years. This growth will not continue indefinitely. The world population is expected to peak at ten billion people at around the next turn of the century (2100) and then stabilize.[15] It is therefore to be expected that the number of vehicles per 100 inhabitants will also gradually reach a saturation point, after which vehicle production and thus the number of vehicles on the road will stabilize.

Assumption 2: Vehicle production growth will continue until the same ownership level is reached on a global scale as in the European Union today, which is about 68 vehicles per 100 inhabitants.

---

i For example, a linear increase in the growth of your bank balance of $100 by $3 per year means that your bank balance has increased to $103 after one year, to $106 after two years, to $109 after three years, and so on.

ii For example, an exponential increase in the growth of your bank balance of $100 by 3% means that your bank balance increases by 3% from year to year. After one year, your bank balance has increased to $103, after two years to $106.09, after three years to $109.27, and so on.

Stabilization of the world population at ten billion people means that I assume that the number of vehicles will stabilize at about the same number of cars per 100 inhabitants as is currently the case in the European Union. This assumption leads to the outcome that the moment of stabilization of the number of cars at 6.8 billion will be in around 2120; that is, in about a century.

Assumption 3: From 2040, all new vehicles in the world will be electric. This is five years later than in the European Union.

With a linear growth in new vehicles of 2.3 million per year, world vehicle production will be about 141 million in 2040 (all electric cars). Between 2011 and 2023, global electric car production grew from a few tens of thousands to almost 14 million per year (see Figure 1.2). In 2021, one in every ten new cars was already electric.[16] This, therefore, represents more than 1,000-fold growth in just ten years,[17] or an exponential growth rate of 60% per year. As of 2017, China consistently accounts for more than half of electric car sales.

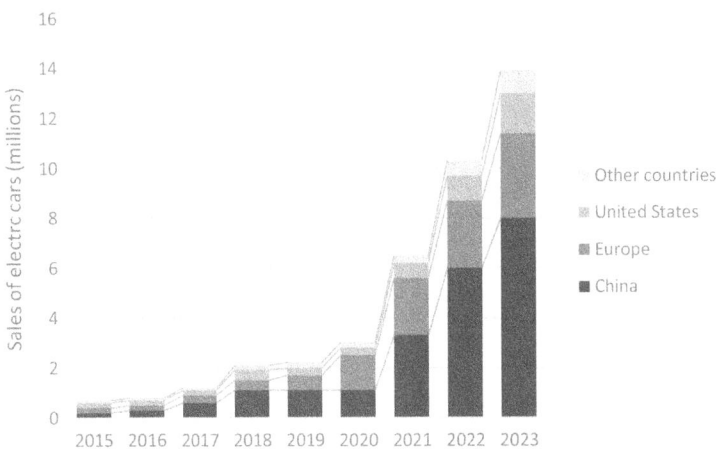

Figure 1.2 Sales of electric cars in the world. Europe includes the EU27, Norway, Iceland, Switzerland, and the United Kingdom. Other countries are Australia, Brazil, Canada, Chile, India, Japan, Korea, Malaysia, New Zealand, Thailand, and South Africa.[17]

Source: International Energy Agency, 2022, Global supply chains of EV batteries. www.iea.org/reports/global-supply-chains-of-ev-batteries.

The growth in sales of new plug-in hybrid cars was roughly the same between 2011 and 2021. However, I assume that sales of plug-in hybrid vehicles will decline again, since the intention is to stop using fossil-fuel-based engines altogether as of 2040. To achieve a production level of 141 million new electric cars by 2040, over 19% more electric cars will have to roll off the assembly line each year between 2023 and 2040. Given the growth rate of the electric car fleet over the past decade, that in itself does not seem to be a problem for car manufacturers. The question, however, is whether the supply of raw materials will be able to keep up with the dramatic increase in demand for electric cars. After all, some of the same raw materials are also needed for other areas of the energy transition, such as the production of solar panels and wind turbines and the expansion of networks for the transmission and distribution of electricity.

As Figure 1.3 shows, the production of new fossil-fuel cars will decrease as more electric cars are produced. I estimate that very few new fossil-fuel cars will be produced in the world after 2040, simply because it is no longer financially interesting for car manufacturers. Starting in 2040, the increase in the number of new electric cars will change from an exponential increase of 19% per year to a linear increase of 2.3 million vehicles per year until market saturation. This means an extrapolation of the straight 'total' line in Figure 1.3 until

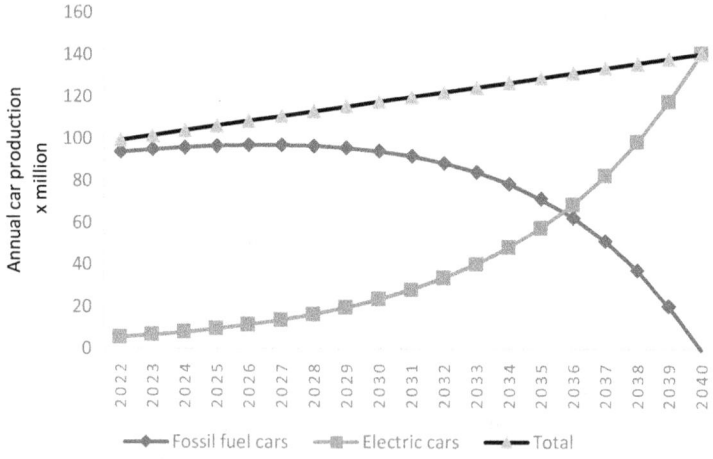

Figure 1.3 Production scenario of fossil-fuel cars and electric cars between 2022 and 2040.

Toward electric driving in a fair world 11

about 2120, after which this line will remain horizontal at a production rate of 272 million new cars per year.

Assumption 4: The average life span of fossil-fuel cars is 20 years and of electric cars 25 years.

Unlike vehicle production statistics, which are reliable because cars are manufactured in a limited number of factories, the number of vehicles on global roads can only be an estimate. Data on the average lifespan of vehicles around the world are unreliable, because records of when a car is permanently discontinued are not equally accurate in all countries. Older cars are also exported on a large scale from richer countries to poorer countries, which may create a difference in vehicles with higher and lower lifespans. This would explain, for example, why the average lifespan of vehicles in the eastern part of Europe is much higher (28 years) than in the more western countries of Europe (18 years).[18] Furthermore, many countries do not levy road tax, such as France, Poland, and the United States, so that people leave their old unused car in the yard for years. The assumption that the average lifespan of fossil-fuel cars is about 20 years implies that there will be almost no more fossil-fuel cars on the road from 2060, when all vehicles will be electric.

The average lifespan of an electric car is expected to be longer than that of a fossil-fuel car because of its simpler construction with far fewer parts. Based on the assumptions regarding the lifespans of fossil-fuel and electric cars, the total number of vehicles on the road will have increased from about 1.4 billion in 2023 to about 2.4 billion by 2040, about one-third of which will be electric cars. The majority of vehicles on the road in 2040 will therefore still be fossil-fuel cars, although most of these will no longer be driving by around 2060 (see Figure 1.4).

Based on the assumptions made regarding production growth and vehicle lifespan, the number of vehicles on the road will continue to grow until around 2120—100 years from now—in the fair scenario, when the number of vehicles per 100 inhabitants globally will be equal to that in the European Union today. This amounts to 6.8 billion vehicles for a world population of ten billion people. With an average lifespan of 25 years for electric cars, 272 million vehicles must be produced annually to stabilize the number of vehicles on the road at 6.8 billion. I assume that further vehicle production growth

12 Toward electric driving in a fair world

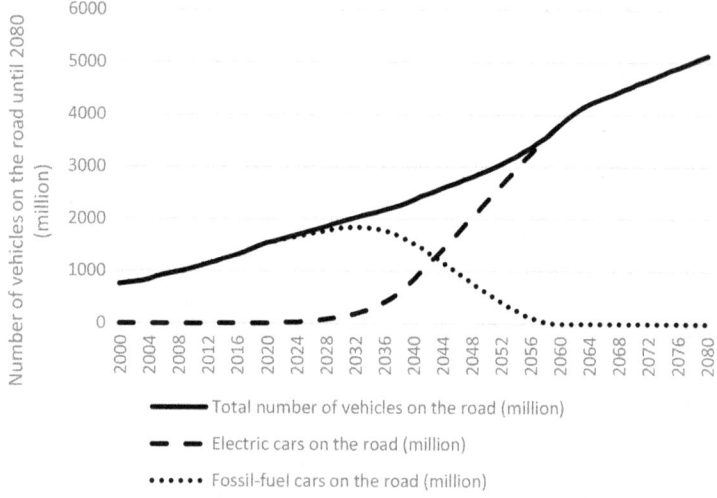

Figure 1.4 Estimate of the total number of vehicles and number of fossil-fuel and electric vehicles on the road worldwide.

will stop once a production level of about 272 million vehicles per year is reached, which will be around the turn of the century (2100). A production level of 272 million vehicles per year is a factor of 2.7 times higher than today. While this does not seem impossible in terms of production capacity, the question is whether enough raw materials will be available. After all, the quantities of copper, lithium, nickel, cobalt, and rare earths needed for the electric car are much greater than those currently needed in the fossil-fuel car, as I will show in Chapters 2 and 3. Figure 1.5 provides an overview of annual car production and the total number of cars on the road under the fair scenario.

In this book, I ask the following questions:

- In Chapter 2: Will there be enough resources available to permanently supply a future world population of ten billion with electric cars at a level equal to that in the European Union today, which is nearly seven vehicles for every ten inhabitants?
- In Chapter 3: What is the risk that the supply of essential raw materials will be hampered due to geopolitical problems or that the

Toward electric driving in a fair world 13

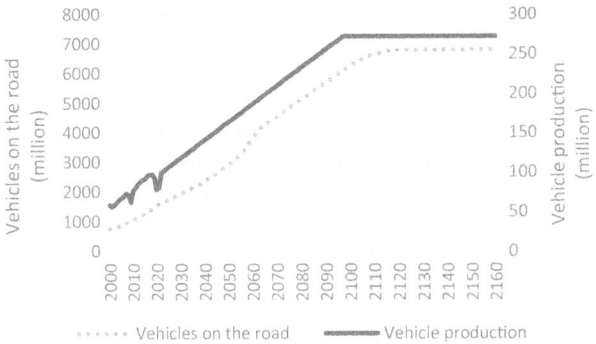

Figure 1.5 Vehicles on the road and annual vehicle production in the fair scenario.

capacity of the mines where these raw materials are mined cannot be scaled up quickly enough?
- In Chapter 4: How sensitive is the outcome of Chapters 2 and 3 to the assumptions made?
- In Chapter 5: What uses do the five metals that may pose availability problems have beyond electric cars? Which companies and countries are involved in their production? Where are the main remaining reserves? What possibilities exist for substitution and recycling?
- In Chapter 6: What will the impact of the transition from fossil-fuel cars to electric cars be on the recycling of scrap cars?
- In Chapter 7: How can the market be put at the service of a fair resource management?

> *Will Max Verstappen usher in a new era of fossil-free race cars, or will Formula 1 races continue to exist as a relic of the fossil era? Max Verstappen's car now uses about 45 liters of fuel to drive 100 kilometers.*[19] *While this is almost one liter of fuel for every two kilometers, Verstappen's car is already much more fuel-efficient than Formula 1 cars were 20 years ago, when 80 liters of fuel were needed to drive 100 kilometers. The main rationale for making race cars more fuel-efficient has nothing to do with the environmental concerns of racing organizers, but with the lower weight of the cars achieved in this way, making*

them faster. It has been agreed that, starting in 2030, race cars will run on fully synthetic fuel,[20] allowing for CO_2-neutral racing. Formula E races have been taking place since 2014 with fully electric cars,[21] and under the auspices of the world motorsport federation FIA since 2021.

Notes

1. Strohl, D. 2018. "Ford, Edison and the cheap EV that almost was." *Wired*, June 18. www.wired.com/2010/06/henry-ford-thomas-edison-ev/
2. Thomas Edison. 2023. Wikipedia. https://en.wikipedia.org/w/index.php?title=Thomas_Edison&oldid=1153889934
3. "Gaining back the EV revenue stream Henry Ford & Thomas Edison gave up." https://cleantechnica.com/2019/02/17/gaining-back-the-ev-revenue-stream-henry-ford-and-thomas-edison-gave-up/
4. Strohl, D. 2018. "Ford, Edison and the cheap EV that almost was." *Wired*, June 18. www.wired.com/2010/06/henry-ford-thomas-edison-ev/
5. Giesen, P. 2023. *Autopia*. Alphabet Publishers.
6. Giesen, P. 2023. *Autopia*. Alphabet Publishers.
7. Van Wingerden, J. 2022. "Global EV sales rise sharply, BYD largest manufacturer," *Autoweek*, August 11.
8. Shepardson, D. and Mason J., 2022. "Biden hops into Corvette, declares Detroit 'back' at EV-focused auto show," Reuters, September 15.
9. Seba T., 2014. *Clean Disruption of Energy and Transportation: How Silicon Valley Will Make Oil, Nuclear, Natural Gas, Coal, Electric Utilities and Conventional Cars Obsolete by 2030*. Lightning Source, La Vergne, TN.
10. United Nations Department of Economic and Social Affairs, 2019, Revision of World Population Prospects, 2019. https://population.um.org/wpp, December 16, 2021.
11. Bardi, U. and Pereira, A., 2022. *Limits and Beyond: 50 Years on from the Limits to Growth, What Did We Learn and What's Next*. Exapt Press, Rotherham, England.
12. Association de Constructeurs Européens d'Automobiles, https://fr.wikipedia.org/wiki/Association_des_constructeurs_europ%C3%A9ens_d%27automobiles; December 29, 2021.
13. International Organization of Motor Vehicle Manufacturers, www.oica.net/production-statistics/, accessed August 15, 2022.
14. *Transportation Energy Data Book*, various editions, US Department of Energy, August 19, 2022.
15. United Nations Department of Economic and Social Affairs, 2019, Revision of World Population Prospects, 2019. https://population.um.org/wpp, December 16, 2021.

16 International Energy Agency, 2022, Global Supply Chains of EV Batteries. www.iea.org/reports/global-supply-chains-of-ev-batteries
17 "Global EV Outlook 2022: Securing Supplies for an Electric Future." 2022. https://iea.blob.core.windows.net/assets/e0d2081d-487d-4818-8c59-69b638969f9e/GlobalElectricVehicleOutlook2022.pdf, August 13.
18 Held, M., Rosat, N., Georges, G., Pengg, H., and Boulouchos, K., 2021. Lifespans of passenger cars in Europe: empirical modeling of fleet turnover dynamics, *European Transport Research Review*, vol. 13.
19 GPFans, "How much fuel does a Formula 1 car consume during a race," October 19, 2022. www.gpfans.com/nl/f1-nieuws/94024/hoeveel-brandstof-verbruikt-een-formule-1auto-tijdens-een-race/#:~:text=Verbruik%20 Formule%201%2Dauto's&text=Een%20Grand%20Prix%20wordt%20v erreden,voor%20een%20race%20wordt%20gebruikt
20 Adenauer, K., 2021. Formula 1 cuts knot: no electric, but synthetic e-fuels, *Autobahn*, October 5.
21 RN 365, 2023. "Formula E—Everything you need to know about the electric racing class," https://racingnews365.nl/formule-e-alles-wat-je-moet-weten-over-de-elektrische-raceklasse, accessed May 15.

2 Protecting climate may bite resources conservation

Governments, many car drivers, and certainly the automotive industry are in no doubt: thanks to the electric (or hydrogen) car, we can keep moving forward for years to come. Simply replace gas stations with charging stations, and the environmental risks of the car are solved. The new car is quiet, clean, and climate-friendly. However, things are not so simple. Even though this story is about raw materials, particularly metals, in the end, it all comes down to energy.

Energy from renewable sources, while undergoing rapid development, is a scarce resource. In 2021, 176,431 TWh[i] of energy were generated worldwide,[1] of which 136,018 TWh, or more than three quarters, from coal, oil, and gas. All this energy will need to be generated by renewable sources within a few decades and, where this is not possible, the greenhouse gases produced by the remaining sources will need to be captured and safely stored. At the same time, global energy demand continues to grow robustly, especially in emerging economies.

The success of the electric car depends not only on whether enough renewable energy can be generated quickly enough to repeatedly charge its batteries but also on whether the raw materials needed in the transition from fossil-fuel to electric cars can be extracted using renewable energy. The extraction and processing of raw materials consumes a lot of energy, not only to mine the ores but also to turn the mined ore into products suitable for further processing, for example from iron ore to steel. It is estimated that about 10% of the world's energy consumption is required to mine metal ore and produce metals

---

i TWh = terawatt-hour; 1 TWh = 1 billion kilowatt-hours (kWh).

DOI: 10.4324/9781003509431-2

from it.[2] Whether all that green energy will be available in a timely and sufficient amount depends on how quickly the necessary wind turbines and solar panels can be built and how quickly the power grid can be upgraded to get that energy to where it is needed. However, wind turbines, solar panels, and the extension of power grids also require a lot of raw materials and thus energy to build or install them. Again, that energy must be produced sustainably. And so it goes on, threatening to become a snake biting its own tail.

The Earth's crust contains enough metals to meet human needs for a long time. Of course, mining companies pick the low-hanging fruit first, and as more resources are mined, the concentration in which they occur decreases, their depth increases, or they are found only in hard-to-access and remote places, such as under the ice of Greenland or at the bottom of the ocean. The remaining fruit hangs ever higher, or rather deeper in the case of mineral resources. This includes metals needed for the energy transition, such as copper, nickel, lithium, cobalt, and rare earths. The result: as resources become more difficult to access, their extraction causes more and more damage to nature and the environment and requires more and more energy, until a limit is reached at which point further extraction is no longer profitable. To give an example, at a certain point the extraction of an additional kilogram of copper will cost more energy than can be produced using that kilogram of copper. The energy investment then exceeds the energy return and extraction stops.

The net amount of energy required to produce an electric car depends mainly on the weight of the car, the type of raw materials in the car, and how much of the raw materials used come from recycled materials. From a climate perspective, it is important that the raw materials for electric cars are produced using climate-neutral energy, and that the battery is charged using clean energy. This, in turn, is relevant to resource use, because additional facilities (solar panels, wind turbines, hydroelectric plants) will have to be built to supply that clean energy, each with their own resource consumption. This is the secondary resource use of the electric car.

> *The heavier a car is, the more energy is used to produce and drive it. The weight of an electric car is on average a lot higher than that of a fossil-fuel car, not only because of the heavy battery but also because people tend to buy bigger cars. Despite*

> the larger and heavier cars, the much more efficient use of energy means that the switch from fossil to electric is still highly beneficial in terms of CO_2 emissions, even if the energy used to produce the car and its batteries and to charge the batteries all comes from fossil fuels.
>
> Mid-range electric cars use about 15–20 kWh per 100 kilometers. Nearly 90% of that energy is used to propel the car. We must realize that with electricity production by a power plant fired by fossil fuel, about 60% of the energy gets lost, which means that the amount of energy necessary to propel an electric car must be multiplied by a factor of two and a half unless the heat produced in the power plant is applied for useful purposes. So not 15–20 kWh per 100 kilometers but 40–50 kWh per 100 kilometers. But that is still substantially less than a mid-range fossil-fuel car using 60–90 kWh per 100 kilometers while transferring only about 20% of the fuel's energy to the wheels. The rest is lost in the car, mostly as heat. The energy consumption of a fossil-fuel car is therefore about four to six times higher than that of an electric car, at least while driving. However, it takes a lot more energy to produce an electric car than a fuel car. In particular, the production of the battery requires more than half of the total energy needed to produce an electric car. That difference is more than made up for during the car's use, except if the electric car is driven very little. Based on the 2023–2040 power mix, the total carbon footprint after driving a fossil-fuel car for 220,000 kilometers is about 2.5 times larger than that of an electric car.[3]

The electric car does not yet look very different from its predecessors. The chassis, bodywork, interior, and wheels remain pretty much the same. On the outside, the electric car is still a combination of metal, rubber, plastic, and glass. The front grill is no longer necessary, as an electric motor does not need to be cooled, and there is no exhaust at the rear, nor is there a catalytic converter to clean the exhaust gases. However, the resource consumption of an electric car is a lot higher than that of a fossil-fuel car. In terms of quantity, the ten main metals in a fuel car are (in alphabetical order): aluminum, chromium, iron, copper, lead, magnesium, manganese, nickel, titanium, and zinc (see Figure 2.1). These are not the only metals in a car. More than 40 other

Protecting climate may bite resources conservation 19

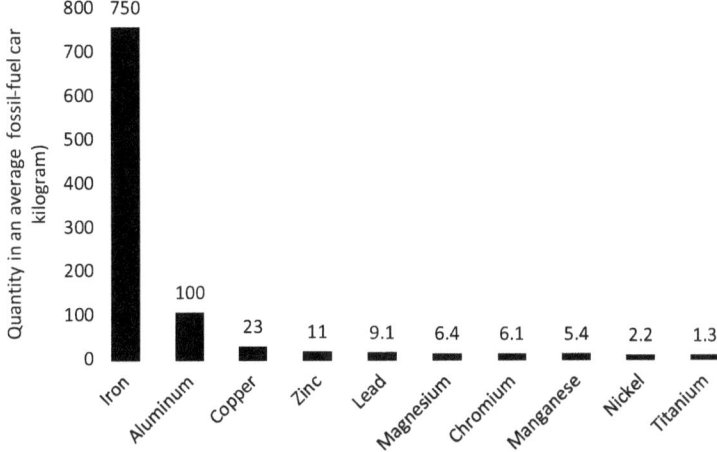

Figure 2.1 The ten main metals in a fossil-fuel car by quantity (for an 'average' car by weight). Only the metals with more than one kilogram in a car are included. The data are from 15 different studies.

Sources: Cullbrand, K. and Magnusson, O., 2012. The use of potentially critical materials in passenger cars, Chalmers University of Technology, Report no 2012:13; Ortego, A., Valero, Al, Valero, An, and Restrepa, E., 2018. Vehicles and critical raw materials, *Journal of Industrial Ecology*, 22(5), 1005–1015; Valero, Al, Valero, An, Calvo, G., and Ortego, A., 2018. Material bottlenecks in the future development of green technologies, *Renewable and Sustainable Energy Reviews*, 93, 178–200; Valero, Al, Valero, An, and Calvo, G., 2021. *The Material Limits of Energy Transition: Thanatia*, Springer, New York; World Bank Group, 2017. The growing role of minerals and metals for a low carbon future, https://documents.worldbank.org/en/publication/documents-reports/documentdetail/207371500386458722/the-growing-role-of-minerals-and-metals-for-a-low-carbon-future; González Palencia, J.C., Sakamaki, T., Araki, M., and Shiga, S., 2015. Impact of powertrain electrification, vehicle size reduction and lightweight materials substitution on energy use, CO_2 emissions and cost of a passenger light-duty vehicle fleet. *Energy*, 93, 1489–1504; Grandell, L., Lehtilä, A., Kivinen, M., Koljonen, T., Kihlman, S., and Lauri, L.S. 2016. Role of critical metals in the future markets of clean energy technologies. *Renew Energy*, 95, 53–62; Iglesias-Émbil, M., Valero, A., Ortego, A., Villacampa, M., Vilaró, J., and Villalba, G., 2020. Raw material use in a battery electric car—a thermodynamic rarity assessment, *Resources, Conservation and Recycling*, 158, 104820; Ortego, A., Valero,Al., Valero, An., Iglesias, M., 2018. Downcycling in automobile recycling process: a thermodynamic assessment, *Resources, Conservation and Recycling*, 136, 24–32; Bhuwalka, K., Field, F.R., De Kleine, R.D., Kim, H.C., Wallington, T.J., and Kirchain R.E., 2021. Characterizing the changes in material use due to vehicle electrification, *Environmental Science and Technology*, 55, 10097–10107; Field, F.R., Wallington, T.J., Everson, M., and Kirchain, R.E., 2017. Strategic materials in the automobile: a comprehensive assessment of strategic and minor metals use in passenger cars and light trucks, *Environmental Science & Technology*, 51, 14436–14444; Huisman, J., Leroy, P., Tertre, F., Södermann, M.L.,

Figure 2.1 (Continued)

Chancerel, P., Cassard, D., Lovik, A.N., Wäger, P., Kushnir, D., Rotter, V.S., Mählitz, P., Herreras, L., Emmench, J., Hallberg, A., Habib, H., Wagner, M., and Downes, S., 2017. Prospecting secondary raw materials in the urban mine and mining wastes ProSUM, Final Report; Xu, G., Yano, J., and Sakai, S., 2016. Scenario analysis for recovery of rare earth elements from end-of-life vehicles, *Journal of Material Cycles and Waste Management*, 18, 469–482; Alonso, E., Wallington, T., Sherman, A., Everson, M., Field, F., Roth, R., and Kirchain, R., 2012. An assessment of the rare earth element content of conventional and electric vehicles, *SAE International Journal of Materials and Manufacturing*, 5(2), 473–477); The role of critical minerals in clean energy transitions, World Energy Outlook, Special Report, 2021. www.iea.org/reports/the-role-of-critical-minerals-in-clean-energy-transitions.

metals are used, all in quantities of less than one kilogram per car. In addition, an average car contains about 280 kilograms of plastics, 50 kilograms of glass, and 40 kilograms of rubber. This is a long list and includes metals whose geological exhaustion is imminent or that may become temporarily scarce for geopolitical reasons.

These scarcity problems will not disappear when switching to the electric car, as it too contains the aforementioned metals in roughly the same quantities as the traditional fuel car. Admittedly, some metals used in a fuel car are no longer needed, such as platinum and palladium, which are mainly used in catalytic converters to clean the exhaust gases. Focusing on metals that total more than one kilogram in an average car, the electric car contains three new metals (cobalt, lithium, and rare earths), and four metals that are used in much greater quantities than in the fuel car (aluminum, barium, copper, and nickel). The bulk of these additional metals are used in the batteries and electric motor: copper and rare earths in the electric motor, and nickel, lithium, cobalt, and—again—copper in the batteries. Aluminum is used in the construction of battery packs and to replace steel to make the electric car lighter. Barium compounds are used as a magnetic material in electric motors and in supercapacitors to store electrical energy when braking and release it when accelerating.

Much of the increase in the use of raw materials in electric cars is for the traction battery. The chemical composition and size and weight of a traction battery are determined by the requirements for such a battery, which concern

- the car's range, which is currently a minimum of 300 to 400 kilometers;

- the number of charging cycles over the life of the battery: the battery should be able to be recharged often before the quality deteriorates too far;
- the battery weight, which should not be too high: this is expressed as energy density, or the amount of energy that can be stored, expressed in kWh per kilogram of battery;
- the power output, which is the tractive force that can be delivered to the electric motor;
- the battery safety: this mainly concerns limiting fire hazards;
- the price of the raw materials;
- the availability of raw materials.

Traction batteries are designed to propel electric cars. The chemistry is quite different from that of lead-acid batteries, which are used to start the car and operate the lights and other electrically powered components of a fuel car. The traction batteries in electric cars are based on lithium-ion technology, which was first used in small batteries in the 1980s. Lithium-ion batteries combine high energy density with a high number of charge cycles. The energy density of a lithium-ion battery is as much as a factor of three to six times that of a lead-acid battery. Electric cars currently combine both types of batteries: the traction battery, which provides the drive for the electric motor, and a 12-volt lead battery, which—as in the classic car— controls the lights, electronics, and other systems such as the brake and power steering, the windshield wipers, the locks, and the windows. The 12-volt battery in an electric car is no longer needed to start the engine and is therefore somewhat smaller than the lead battery in a fuel car. The traction battery operates a high-voltage system of up to 800 volts. It is quite conceivable that the separate 12-volt system will disappear from the electric car in the future and that the lithium-ion battery pack will be used for everything, but this will not happen in the short term as it is currently too expensive to develop the many new components. The traction battery charges the 12-volt battery using an inverter.

The cost of an electric car is largely determined by the cost of the battery. Currently, the cost of the batteries in a C-segment electric car still accounts for about 40% of the manufacturing cost.[4] This will be more for smaller cars with the same range and less for more expensive cars. In Europe, the manufacturing cost of a car is about 60%–65% of its selling price (before taxes). C-class cars include the Audi A3, BMW 1, Citroen C4, Opel Astra, Renault Megane, Toyota Corolla, and Volkswagen Golf. The cost of car batteries continues to decline year on year. The manufacturing cost of electric cars is expected to become less than that of their fuel counterparts sometime between 2025 and 2030, after which subsidies to promote electric car sales will no longer be needed. It is expected that the cost of car batteries in a C-segment car will then have fallen to about 30% of the car manufacturing costs.[5]

The cost of a battery is mainly determined by its capacity; in other words, how many kilowatt-hours the charged battery can accommodate. Together with the weight of the car, this determines the range of an electric car. Car battery prices have dropped by a factor of about five in the last ten years, from $732 (at 22$[ii]) per kWh in 2013 to $151 (at 22$) per kWh in 2022.[6] There was no decrease between 2021 and 2022 due to the increase in commodity prices caused by a combination of the war in Ukraine and high demand for certain raw materials due to the energy transition. However, battery prices are expected to continue to decline, although perhaps with some delay. The cost of a 50-kWh battery pack was about $7,500 in 2022, and the electricity consumption of a C-segment car is about 1 kWh for every 6–7 km.

The first step in the discovery of the lithium-ion battery was made as early as the 1970s by the 35-year-old Briton Stanley Whittingham. He was working at Exxon at the time and was the author of the first publication in 1976 on a new type of battery based on lithium ions. The American John Goodenough succeeded in doubling the capacity of the battery in the Chemistry Laboratory at Oxford University in 1980. Then, following further improvements, the lithium-ion battery was commercialized by Sony based on work by the Japanese Akira Yoshino, who was

ii 22$ represents the purchasing power of one U.S. dollar in 2022.

able to create the first prototype of a rechargeable lithium-ion battery in 1983. Stanley Whittingham, John Goodenough, and Akira Yoshino received the Nobel Prize in Chemistry in 2019 for their work that led to the development and realization of the lithium-ion battery.

A battery pack consists of several battery modules—perhaps ten—which contain the individual battery cells. Each battery cell consists of a cathode containing active material, such as lithium, nickel, cobalt, and manganese, and an anode, such as graphite. The cathode and anode are separated by an electrolyte. In the case of lithium-ion batteries, the electrolyte consists of a mixture of flammable organic liquids that conducts lithium ions from the cathode to the anode. This creates an electric current, which is dissipated through a current collector, usually made of copper.

Technical developments in the battery are multiple and taking place rapidly, on every front: the weight is decreasing, the energy density and lifespan are increasing, the cost is falling, and the battery is getting safer. As for the use of raw materials, there is a choice. Different types of lithium-ion batteries are referred to by the names of the elements in the battery's cathode. These include the following:

- lithium cobalt oxide (LCO)
- lithium manganese oxide (LMO)
- lithium nickel cobalt aluminum (NCA)
- lithium nickel manganese cobalt aluminum (NMC)
- lithium iron phosphate (LFP)

The cathode

The variants of NMC (nickel manganese cobalt) batteries are currently the favorites among electric car manufacturers, as they couple high energy density (140–200 Wh/kg) with a long life (1,000–2,000 cycles). The nickel cobalt aluminum (NCA) battery has a higher energy density (200–250 Wh/kg) and is, therefore, smaller and lighter for the same amount of energy content but has a shorter lifespan. The NCA battery also has a high specific power. It is more expensive than NMC batteries and is mainly used in the more expensive electric car segment.

NMC and NCA batteries both have the disadvantage of containing cobalt and nickel, which are expensive. Cobalt also has the disadvantage that about 70% of it is mined in the Democratic Republic of Congo (partly using child labor), so its supply is considered uncertain. However, the less cobalt is used in an NMC battery, the more nickel it needs.

LFP (lithium iron phosphate) batteries couple high thermal stability with lower cost than the other types of batteries, due to their cheaper chemistry, and have a very long life of up to 2,000 charge cycles. However, they have a lower energy density that is two-thirds of that of NMC batteries and only half that of NCA batteries. While LFP batteries do not contain nickel and cobalt, making them cheaper than the other batteries and making production less uncertain both in the short and long term, they do however contain 50% more copper than NCA and NMC batteries. The Chinese car manufacturer BYD is marketing cars with LFP batteries (the BYD Atto 3), and Tesla and Volkswagen have also announced that they will use LFP batteries in some of their new types of electric cars.

LCO (lithium cobalt oxide) batteries have a high energy density but are less thermally stable than the other battery types and have a shorter lifespan (i.e., fewer charging cycles) and are therefore not used in vehicles.

LMO (lithium manganese oxide) batteries are more thermally stable than LCO batteries, have a longer service life, a high specific power, and do not contain cobalt. However, they have a lower energy density at about two-thirds of that of the LCO battery. The same amount of energy therefore requires a 30% heavier (and larger) battery compared to an LCO battery. This type of battery is used in electric bicycles.

The anode

Graphite has been the preferred choice of lithium-ion producers so far, but other anode compositions are also being explored.

Protecting climate may bite resources conservation 25

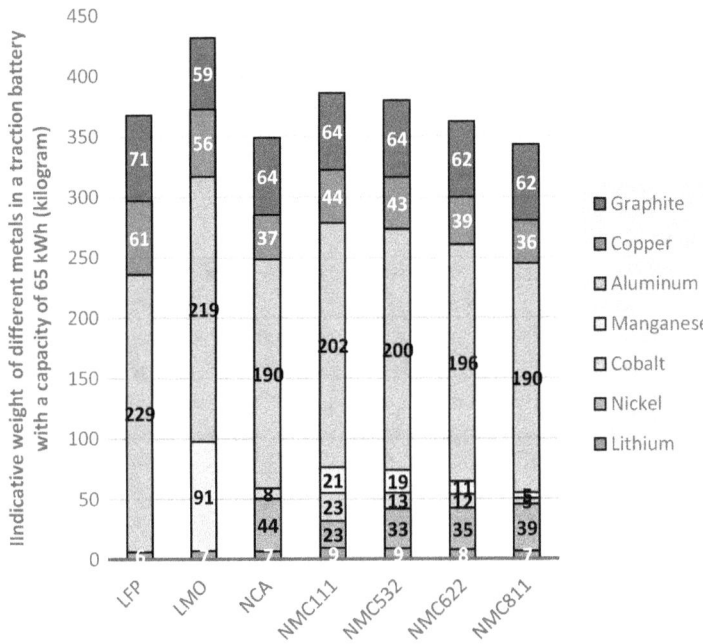

Figure 2.2 Weight of components of different types of batteries, each of 65 kWh. NMC = nickel manganese cobalt, NCA = nickel cobalt aluminum, LMO = lithium manganese oxide, and LFP = lithium iron phosphate. The numbers after NMC indicate the weight ratio of nickel, manganese, and cobalt (Dunn, J., Slattery, M., Kendall, A., Ambrose, H., and Shen, S., 2021. Circularity of lithium-ion battery materials in electric vehicles. *Environment, Science and Technology*, 55, 5189–5198.). *Note*: Not all materials are included, for example, iron and phosphate in the LFP battery, oxygen in all batteries, and the various components that make up the electrolyte. The longest piece of column in the middle of each rod is aluminum. Above that are copper and graphite, respectively, and below that are manganese, cobalt, nickel, and lithium as the bottom block, respectively. Nickel and cobalt are not included in LFP and LMO batteries.

In 2020, the market share of various types of NMC batteries was still dominant, at 72%. The market share of NCA batteries was 20%, that of LMO batteries 6%, and that of LFP batteries 2%.[7] However, LFP batteries are rapidly emerging.

The amounts of metals in various types of batteries vary quite a bit (see Figure 2.2). I take a 65-kWh battery as an example because this capacity can be considered average. The total weight of a 65-kWh battery is currently approximately 450–520 kg, or 7–8 kg per kWh of storage capacity.

It is notable that, despite being called a lithium-ion battery, the amount of lithium is relatively small, at about 6–9 kg, or about 1–2% of the total weight of the battery. Also notable is the comparatively large proportion of aluminum; about half of the battery's weight. Except for the NCA and NMC batteries, aluminum is used purely for structural purposes.

Battery manufacturers are reaching theoretical limits in terms of the energy density of the above battery types. To further increase energy density, much research is being done on the possibilities of 'all solid-state batteries' (ASSBs). The fundamental difference is that ASSBs have a solid electrolyte instead of the flammable liquid electrolyte found in current lithium-ion batteries. ASSBs are therefore much safer than 'traditional' lithium-ion batteries and do not require cooling.

> *The importance of fire safety was demonstrated by the great outcry caused by the fire on the car carrier the* Tremantle Highway *in July 2023 off the Dutch Wadden Islands. The ship was transporting about 4,000 cars, 500 of which were electric. Furthermore, some associations of owners in the Netherlands have banned the parking of electric cars in parking garages under their residential complexes as a precaution (NOS News, November 28, 2021), and rechargeable batteries are banned as checked baggage on airplanes.*

The absence of a liquid electrolyte also makes the production process simpler. Moreover, the great advantage of ASSBs is that the energy density is much higher than that of current lithium-ion batteries: up to 70% higher, and potentially up to 480 Wh/kg.[8] However, the ASSB has not yet outgrown the laboratory and prototype stage, and there are still many steps to take before large-scale production. It may be possible in the future to replace the NMC cathodes now mostly used in the ASSB experiments with a lithium sulfur cathode, and additionally to apply silver carbon as anode material instead of lithium metal, theoretically increasing the energy density of the ASSB even further. The

International Energy Agency expects ASSBs to be used in electric cars no sooner than the early 2030s.[9]

> The world's largest producer of lithium-ion batteries for electric cars, stationary battery storage systems, and battery management systems is China's Contemporary Amperex Technology Co. Ltd (CATL). The energy storage capacity of batteries produced by CATL was about 100 gigawatt-hours in 2021, about one-third of total world production in that year. CATL plans to increase that capacity fivefold by 2025. CATL has only existed since 2012 and was able to grow into the global player it is today in such a short time thanks in part to subsidies from the Chinese state and to German and Japanese technology.[10]

The shift in the metal spectrum has major implications. No matter how clean and economical an electric car is while driving, the drain on the finite supply of metals in the Earth's crust is, on average, much more than that of fossil-fuel car production. In addition, due to the increasing number of cars, the raw material consumption of cars could eventually become as much as four times higher than today. This is especially true for metals that were hardly used in traditional cars: lithium, cobalt, and rare earths, but also for metals of which an electric car contains substantially more than a fuel car, such as copper, nickel, and aluminum.

As mentioned above, a modern car contains more than 50 different metals. Of course, the absolute amount per vehicle depends on the vehicle's total weight, with an SUV containing from two to as much as four times the amount of each metal in a small car. Of these more than 50 metals, I have selected 15 metals for which demand will increase significantly with the electrification of vehicles (see Table 2.1). The numbers are averages, based on current battery technology and a mid-size car. I have also indicated in Table 2.1 which of these metals are among the scarcest metals[iii] in the Earth's crust, and which are considered critical by the European Commission.

---

iii Scarcity is here meant as relative scarcity, that is, the amount of economically exploitable material in the Earth's crust relative to the annual extraction rate and its increase.

Table 2.1 Metals that are significantly more prevalent in electric cars than in fuel cars

Metal	Quantity in average electric car (kg per car)	Belongs to the 11 scarcest metals	Appears on the European Commission's list of critical raw materials[b]	Average weight increase in an electric car compared to a fuel car with current battery technology (%)
Aluminum/Bauxite	190		X	90
Antimony	0.13	X	X	170
Barium/Barite	1.6		X	320
Boron	0.057	X	X	94
Cobalt	7.4		X	27,000
Copper	120	X	X	420
Lithium	7.0		X	79,000
Molybdenum	0.41	X		64
Nickel, battery grade	50	X	X	2,200
Niobium	0.31		X	107
Strontium	0.33		X	74
Rare earths[a]	1.1		X	3,200
Silver	0.025	X		67
Tantalum	0.011		X	100
Vanadium	0.47		X	120

Notes: The list only includes metals that appear in the European Commission's list of critical raw materials and/or are among the 11 scarcest metals. The sources are the same as used in Figure 2.1.

[a] In vehicles, these are mainly dysprosium (210 g), neodymium (770 g), praseodymium (100 g), samarium (3.2 g), terbium (15 g), ytterbium (0.16 g).
[b] European Commission, 2023. Proposal for a Regulation of the European Parliament and of the Council establishing a framework for ensuring a secure and sustainable supply of critical raw materials and amending Regulations (EU)168/2013. (EU) 2018/858, 2018/1724 and (EU) 2019/1020, COM(2023)160final 2023/0079(COD), March 16, 2023.

On March 16, 2023, the European Commission unveiled its Critical Raw Materials Act, which contains a list of 34 critical raw materials. These are raw materials that are not produced in the European Union, or in very low quantities, but that are important for the economies of the Member States and for which the security of supply is comparatively low. The security of supply of a raw material is qualified as comparatively low if it is mostly produced in only a few countries outside the EU, especially if those countries also have autocratic or weak governance. The purpose of the Critical Raw Materials Act is to reduce the dependency of the European Union on other countries as far as the supply of these critical raw materials is concerned.

The global consumption of the 15 metals that are much more abundant in electric cars than in fossil-fuel cars (see overview in Table 2.1) is growing not only because of the switch from fossil-fuel to electric driving but also because of their applications, for example, in infrastructure, washing machines, and homes; in short, in all the material things we consume. The capacity for further growth in the number of cars will therefore be determined not only by the material consumption of cars but also by the simultaneous demand for the same materials for other products. If the growth in the use of a particular metal in cars is comparatively small compared to its use elsewhere, the switch from fuel cars to electric cars will have less of an impact on future resource supply.

I now divide the 15 metals into two, overlapping, groups:

(1) Six geologically scarce metals, whose depletion is imminent in the longer term. These are antimony, boron, copper, molybdenum, nickel, and silver.
(2) Thirteen critical metals, whose supply may be disrupted in the short term. Four of these are also geologically scarce: antimony, boron, copper, and nickel.

The environmental impact of resource extraction relates mainly to the large-scale degradation of the landscape, especially in the case of the surface mining of metals, to the enormous consumption of water, and to the gigantic amount of waste. When metal ores are further processed, air pollution as well as water pollution and chemical waste are points of concern. An average electric car contains 120 kilograms of copper. To produce that amount of copper requires 100 to 200 times the amount of ore, that is, about 15–20 tons. This represents a full truck of mining waste for each electric car. Bear in mind, this is only the waste from producing the copper in the car.

In this chapter, I focus on the six geologically scarce metals and the electric car's contribution to their depletion. The key question is whether the fair scenario is feasible as far as these metals are concerned, and, if so, for how long.

Not all resources are equally scarce, as this depends on how much is extracted from the ground each year in relation to the extractable quantity in the Earth's crust. Lower and higher estimates have been made of the extractable quantities of various metals.[11] For some metals, the highest and lowest estimate are far apart, for others much less so. However, the highest estimates of the extractable quantity of metals in the Earth's crust are usually optimistic.

It is important to realize that the term "extractable" in this context is not absolute. "Extractable" means "economically extractable," not "technically extractable." Metals are mined from metal ore, in which the metal content is much higher than the average content of the metal in the Earth's crust. This difference is expressed as the enrichment factor. The enrichment factor of many ores (e.g., copper, nickel, zinc, gold, lead, and tin) is more than 100 and can be as high as 10,000, although the ores of some common metals have a much lower enrichment factor (e.g., aluminum, iron, and titanium). Of course, the total amount of a metal in the Earth's crust is much higher than the amount of that metal in just its ores, as ores make up a very small fraction of the Earth's crust. While it is theoretically possible to continue to extract a metal from the Earth's crust when the ores are depleted, this is highly unlikely because of the enormous energy costs and the gigantic environmental impact of such extraction. From a certain point on, the costs become greater than the yields.

Besides the absolute extractable quantity of a metal in the Earth's crust, a second factor that determines the scarcity of a metal is the rate of increase (or decrease) of the annual extraction of that metal. This can vary from metal to metal. Right now, for example, production rates of metals important to the energy transition are rising faster than those of other metals. There are also metals whose production rates vary considerably. For example, the annual production of antimony increased by almost 3% per year for a long time but has decreased significantly in the last five years. It is not clear whether this will be a temporary decline or not. Table 2.2 provides an indication of the geological scarcity of 33 metals. Note that Table 2.2 is intended to provide an indication of future scarcity: things could turn out better but also worse. So, what does the table show us? We mainly need to be concerned about the metals at the top of the table when it comes to depletion: copper, antimony, boron, silver, bismuth, molybdenum, indium, chromium, zinc, and nickel. I have not included gold, as a lot of all the gold ever mined is still available in gold bars, jewelry, and coins. While delving for new gold may become increasingly difficult and costly as it is still only found at great depths and/or at very low concentrations in the Earth's crust, there is ample gold available above ground for the time being.

Regarding the six geologically scarce metals, antimony is mainly used in flame retardants in plastics, and electric cars contain more plastic than fuel cars. Boron is used to reinforce steel. Copper and nickel are both essential to the success of the energy transition: copper for the transmission and distribution of electricity and in electric motors and electric vehicle (EV) batteries, and nickel in EV batteries. Silver is an essential raw material in electronics, and molybdenum is important for the preparation of high-quality stainless steel. The main producing countries are (in 2022): Chile for copper (27% of world production), Mexico for silver (23% of world production), China for antimony and molybdenum (55% and 45% of world production, respectively), Indonesia for nickel (37% of world production), and Turkey for boron (74% of world production).

Table 2.3 shows the distribution of the use of the six scarce metals under the fair scenario. The table includes three use categories: in electric cars, in other energy transition applications, and in all other applications. We see that the use of antimony, copper, and especially nickel in electric vehicles could substantially increase the consumption of these metals. For nickel, this depends on the battery scenario. We also see that only copper plays a proportionally large role in the other energy transition applications.

The energy transition will be responsible for 34% of the world's nickel use if battery scenario 1 is followed, almost entirely for batteries in electric cars. As for copper, the energy transition will be responsible for 27% of total copper use, about 15% of which will be for electric cars. This does not change much under the various battery scenarios. The rest of the copper will be used mainly for the expansion of electricity transmission and distribution networks. As for antimony, boron, molybdenum, and silver, the energy transition's resource use (including that of the electric car) is small compared to the use of these metals in other applications.

Table 2.2 Indication of the geological scarcity of 33 metals

Metal	Extraction in 2020 (kt)	Indicative estimate of extractable quantity in upper 3 km of the Earth's crust, high estimate (Mt)	Indicative estimate of extractable quantity in upper 3 km of the Earth's crust, low estimate (Mt)	Indicative depletion period (years after 2015)
Copper	20,600	10,000	6,000	100
Antimony	111	100	20	150
Gold	3.0	2	0.3	150
Boron[a]	1,700	3,000	2,000	150
Silver	23.5	20	8	150
Bismuth	18.9	20	6	150
Molybdenum	298	200	200	200
Indium	0.96	30	0.4	250
Chrome	12,800	35,000	10,000	350
Zinc	12,000	30,000	9,000	400
Nickel	2,510	8,000	1,000	450
Tungsten	78.4	200	200	600
Tin	264	300	300	650
Rhenium	0.059	0.1	0.1	700
Selenium	3.1	6	5	700
Cadmium	24	40	30	850
Iron	1,500,000	6,000,000	2,000,000	1,100
Cobalt	142	3,000	200	1,100

Protecting climate may bite resources conservation

Metal				
Platinum group metals[b]	0.383	3	0.9	1,200
Manganese	18,900	100,000	100,000	1,350
Lead	4,400	20,000	2,000	1,500
Lithium	82.5	2,000	500	1,600
Niobium	67.7	2,000	80	1,700
Arsenic	45.4	200	unavailable	4,500
Gallium	0.327	2,000	unavailable	5,100
Rare earths[c]	240	20,000	3,000	5,300
Strontium	350	40,000	9,000	5,400
Aluminum	65,100	10,000,000	200,000	10,500
Titanium[d]	5,156	600,000	10,000	24,000
Tantalum	2.1	200	5	29,500
Vanadium	105	20,000	600	40,000
Magnesium	9,000	3,000,000	70,000	40,000
Germanium	0.14	200	unavailable	550,000

Notes: The figures in the three right-hand columns are taken from a publication by the author (Henckens, T., 2021. *Governance of the World's Mineral Resources. Beyond the Foreseeable Future*, Elsevier, Amsterdam). The 2020 extraction figures are from the U.S. Geological Survey (Mineral Commodity Summaries 2022). The indicative depletion period is based on the high estimate of the extractable quantity of the metal in the upper three kilometers of the Earth's crust, assuming the average outcome of two growth scenarios: (1) a scenario in which growth in annual production of the metal between 1980 and 2015 continues until 2050, halves until 2100, then stops; and (2) a scenario in which the growth in annual production of the metal between 1980 and 2015 continues until 2100, then halves until 2200, then stops.

[a] 2017.
[b] The platinum group metals are platinum, palladium, osmium, iridium, rhodium, and ruthenium.
[c] The rare earth metals are scandium, yttrium, lanthanum, cerium, praseodymium, neodymium, samarium, europium, gadolinium, terbium, dysprosium, holmium, erbium, thulium, ytterbium, lutetium, and promethium.
[d] Ilmenite plus rutile.

Table 2.3 Distribution of net annual use of six scarce metals for different application categories after realization of the fair scenario

	Net annual consumption for the production of new electric cars after completion of the fair scenario, assuming current recycling rates (percentage of total consumption)	Net annual consumption for the rest of the energy transition (solar panels, wind turbines, power grids, and batteries for storage) after completion of the fair scenario, assuming current recycling rates (percentage of total consumption)	Net annual use for other uses after completion of the fair scenario, assuming current recycling rates (percentage of total consumption)
Antimony	9%	0%	91%
Boron	0%	0%	100%
Copper[a]			
Battery scenario 1	17%	10%	73%
Battery scenario 2	16%	11%	73%
Battery scenario 3	17%	10%	73%
Battery scenario 4	19%	10%	71%
Battery scenario 5	14%	11%	75%
Molybdenum	7%	5%	88%
Nickel[a]			
Battery scenario 1	35%	1%	64%
Battery scenario 2	33%	1%	66%
Battery scenario 3	21%	2%	77%
Battery scenario 4	2%	2%	96%
Battery scenario 5	2%	2%	96%
Silver	3%	1%	96%

Notes: [a]Battery scenario 1: Extrapolation of current average battery composition.; Battery scenario 2: 100% NCA batteries.; Battery scenario 3: 100% NMC111 batteries.; Battery scenario 4: 100% LFP batteries.; Battery scenario 5: 100% ASSB batteries with a lithium sulfur cathode and a carbon silver anode.

The premise of the calculations in Table 2.3 and the rest of this book is that annual extraction of the six scarce metals from the Earth's crust will continue to increase at the same rate as in the 40 years from 1980 to 2020. I do this to examine the effect of continued production growth. For almost all metals, growth over the past 40 years has been exponential; in other words, production has increased by the same percentage year on year. Exponential growth obviously cannot continue forever. I therefore assume that the production growth of each metal stops when the world population of ten billion people uses the same amount of that metal as the expected use of the average EU citizen in 2050. Of course, the decline in growth will not be sudden but gradual.

If the current increase in world prosperity compared to EU prosperity continues, the world will have caught up with the European Union (2050) sometime between 2100 and 2150. Of course, this is theoretical. The unexpected can happen, such as—in a negative sense—disasters and large-scale wars. On the positive side, the recycling of scarce resources could be increased or resources could perhaps be replaced by less scarce alternatives in certain applications.

Table 2.4 shows for how many years recoverable antimony, boron, copper, molybdenum, nickel, and silver are estimated to be still available when there are 6.8 billion vehicles on the world's roads. This situation may be reached in around 2120, as we saw in Chapter 1, so roughly in 100 years. I am not specifically looking at electric cars here. With the assumptions of Chapter 1, it is clear that the situation could become dire for all six metals, but in particular for antimony, copper, and nickel.

Table 2.4 is based on an annual production growth of primary raw materials, which is the average outcome of two scenarios:

Table 2.4 Number of years remaining between 2120 and depletion

	High estimate of the still extractable amounts in the Earth's crust (years)	Low estimate of the still extractable amounts in the Earth's crust (years)
Antimony	70	−50
Boron	60	20
Copper	10	−20
Molybdenum	100	100
Nickel	200	−10
Silver	60	−10

Note: The high and low estimate refer to the two middle columns in Table 2.2.

Scenario 1: The annual production increase of mineral resources between 2015 and 2050 is equal to the average annual production increase between 1980 and 2015; the annual production increase between 2050 and 2100 is half of the assumed annual 2015–2050 production increase; after 2100, no further production increase is assumed.

Scenario 2: The annual production increase of mineral resources between 2015 and 2100 is equal to the average annual production increase between 1980 and 2015; the annual production increase between 2100 and 2200 is half of the assumed annual 2015–2050 production increase; after 2200, no further production increase is assumed.

If the low estimate of the amount of extractable resource is correct, then—without further measures—there will be insufficient antimony, copper, nickel, and silver available in the Earth's crust to even be able to produce 6.8 billion vehicles by 2120. Boron will have 20 years to go after 2120, and molybdenum a century, before they are depleted, which is not a bright outlook either. Based on the low estimate of extractable reserves, four of the six metals considered are problematic. Even assuming the high stockpile estimate for copper, this metal will be depleted within 10 years after 2120.

The fair scenario may therefore not be feasible, and certainly not sustainable, unless timely and drastic measures are taken to limit resource use, starting with the six scarce metals discussed in this chapter. Scarcity caused by depletion in the Earth's crust does not create acute problems, because geological resource depletion is not a clearly visible issue at present. However, it is a creeping problem. As we can see, geological depletion will occur for several automotive raw materials but only over a period of a century. This may take a little longer or shorter, depending on the circumstances. Resource depletion is not a trivial problem; it is real and it will happen. As with climate change, humanity must act now to save future generations from major problems. However, I note an unwillingness to take drastic measures now for the benefit of our grandchildren's generation, if there are no benefits for ourselves. Eliminating dependence as now on Russia in terms of fossil fuels and on China in terms of rare earths are apparently more important motives for taking measures than concerns for future generations.

> *In his book* 2052: A Global Forecast for the Next Forty Years,[12] *the Norwegian Jorgen Randers aptly describes the short-term thinking of politicians and economists:*
>
> …forty years of practical experience and forty years of fighting for sustainability have convinced me that society …indeed tends to choose the cheapest solution. This is the solution where the ratio of benefit to cost is the highest—when disregarding the costs and benefits beyond a time horizon of five years, give or take. This is what the economists call the cost-effective solution. … The short time horizon is a serious challenge if society needs to spend now in order to avoid a problem in the distant future. Short-termism works actively against wise policy… It comes as no surprise to those who know economics that it is 'cost-efficient' to allow the world to collapse from climate damage, as long as the collapse is more than forty years into the future. … It is cheaper to push the world over the cliff than to try to save it.

It is hard to fathom, but the next generation will probably extract more metals from the Earth's crust than all the generations before us combined. An example is copper, whose production has doubled every 25 years for the last 100 years. Exponential growth in the extraction of metals from the Earth's crust is not sustainable, and one metal after another will be depleted in the case of continued exponential growth. If humanity wants to avoid this, it needs to start a massive conservation program as soon as possible.

To go back to the question of energy, about 10% of the energy supply is currently required to mine, transport, and process mineral resources.[13] As the concentration of raw materials in ores becomes lower and as deeper mining is required, energy needs will increase. A halving of ore concentration roughly doubles energy requirements. For example, 13% more copper was produced in Chile in 2010 than in 2001, but this required 50% more energy.[14]

There is enough of every metal in the Earth's crust, the seas, and the solar system to supply a multitude of today's humanity virtually forever. The amount of metals is not the problem. The problem is the amount of energy required to extract the metals from ores of very low concentration, from great depths, or from far away from us in the universe. Once it takes more energy to extract the package of metals needed to build a wind turbine than the amount of energy the wind turbine can generate during its lifetime, the extraction of those metals has become meaningless. What ultimately matters is the Energy Return on Energy Investment (EREI), the ratio of the amount of energy required to produce a given amount of a metal to the amount of energy that can be produced using that same amount of metal. Depletion of a metal is determined not so much by the amount of the metal in the ground, but by the energy it takes to extract it. After reaching the fair scenario, the use of electric energy by 6.8 billion cars will require roughly 10% of total electricity consumption. That means an additional 10% of resources is needed for solar panels, wind turbines, battery storage, and electricity transportation just to run cars. The challenge is to recover as much of these additional resources as possible from raw materials already in circulation, or, even better, to replace them with less scarce resources.

Ecological footprint

The ecological footprint of the extraction of all the raw materials necessary for all future electric cars is of course very important. It cannot be the case that the environmental impacts and greenhouse gas emissions associated with raw material production largely cancel out the environmental benefits of switching from fossil-fuel to electric cars. Acceptance of the electric car will therefore largely depend on how "clean" the raw material production is. Electric cars do not produce CO_2 during their use, but they do during their production, at least for now. Indeed, in 2023, much of the extraction and processing of raw materials for electric cars is still based on the use of non-renewable energy sources, not to mention the impact of the extraction and processing of the various metal ores on the surrounding landscape and natural environment. In this regard, it is to be expected that the European Union will impose *increasing requirements on the footprint of the raw materials and components of electric cars. Otherwise, the switch from fossil to electric will yield too few environmental benefits. For raw material manufacturers, it will be a challenge to produce their products entirely using renewable energy sources. It is also extremely important that new car battery factories can use green energy.*

Notes

1. "Energy mix." https://ourworldindata.org/energy-mix, accessed May 15, 2023.
2. Bardi, U., 2014, *Extracted. How the Quest for Mineral Wealth Is Plundering the Planet*. Report for the Club of Rome, Chelsea Green Publishing. Original edition in German, Der geplünderte Planet, Oekom Verlag.
3. Milieu Centraal, 2023. www.milieucentraal.nl/duurzaam-vervoer/elektrische-auto/alles-over-elektrische-auto/, accessed April 15, 2023.
4. "Hyperdrive daily: The EV price gap narrows," www.bloomberg.com/news/newsletters/2021-05-25/hyperdrive-daily-the-ev-price-gap-narrows
5. "Hyperdrive daily: The EV price gap narrows," www.bloomberg.com/news/newsletters/2021-05-25/hyperdrive-daily-the-ev-price-gap-narrows
6. Bloomberg NEF, https://about.bnef.com/blog/lithium-ion-battery-pack-prices-rise-for-first-time-to-an-average-of-151-kwh/, Accessed May 15, 2023.
7. International Energy Agency, The role of critical minerals in clean energy transitions, World Energy Outlook, Special Report, 2021. www.iea.org/reports/the-role-of-critical-minerals-in-clean-energy-transitions
8. International Energy Agency, The role of critical minerals in clean energy transitions, World Energy Outlook, Special Report, 2021. www.iea.org/reports/the-role-of-critical-minerals-in-clean-energy-transitions
9. International Energy Agency, The role of critical minerals in clean energy transitions, World Energy Outlook, Special Report, 2021. www.iea.org/reports/the-role-of-critical-minerals-in-clean-energy-transitions
10. "SNE Research: Global xEV battery market exceeded 296 GWh in 2021," https://insideevs.com/news/568640/global-battery-market-2021/
11. Henckens, T., 2021. *Governance of the World's Mineral Resources. Beyond the Foreseeable Future*. Elsevier, Radarweg, Netherlands.
12. Randers, J., 2012. *2052: A Global Forecast for the Next Forty Years*. Chelsea Green Publishing, White River Junction, VA.

13 Bardi, U., 2014, *Extracted. How the Quest for Mineral Wealth Is Plundering the Planet*. Report for the Club of Rome, Chelsea Green Publishing. Original edition in German, Der geplünderte Planet, Oekom Verlag, p.71.
14 Bardi, U., 2014, *Extracted. How the Quest for Mineral Wealth Is Plundering the Planet*. Report for the Club of Rome, Chelsea Green Publishing. Original edition in German, Der geplünderte Planet, Oekom Verlag.

3 The electric car and the energy transition
Conflict or not?

The next three decades will be critical in terms of metal availability. As cars switch from fossil to electric, the goal is to achieve net zero CO_2 emissions by 2050. The question is whether this rapid transition will create problems for the production and supply of the necessary raw materials.

I assume here the International Energy Agency's NZE Scenario, where NZE stands for net zero emissions. The NZE Scenario shows how to achieve net zero CO_2 emissions by 2050, to maintain the likelihood of meeting the goals of the 2015 UN Paris Climate Agreement regarding maximum global warming.

The NZE Scenario consists of a massive switch to renewable energy and at the same time massive energy savings. In this scenario, world energy consumption in 2050 is 10% less than in 2020, while the world's population is expected to increase by almost a quarter over the same period and simultaneously—hopefully—become more prosperous on average. To the extent that fossil fuels are still used, the released CO_2 must be captured and stored, and if that is not possible, it must be compensated for by extracting and storing CO_2 directly from the air. It is an extremely ambitious scenario, but necessary if we are serious about the Paris goals. The resulting energy mix is shown in Figure 3.1.

The growth in the amount of resources needed for the energy transition is enormous, and the switch from fossil-fuel cars to electric cars will be added in the same period.

I assume that, from 2040, all new vehicles in the world will be electric. In this respect, Europe is leading the way. On October 27, 2022, the European Parliament and the European Council agreed

DOI: 10.4324/9781003509431-3

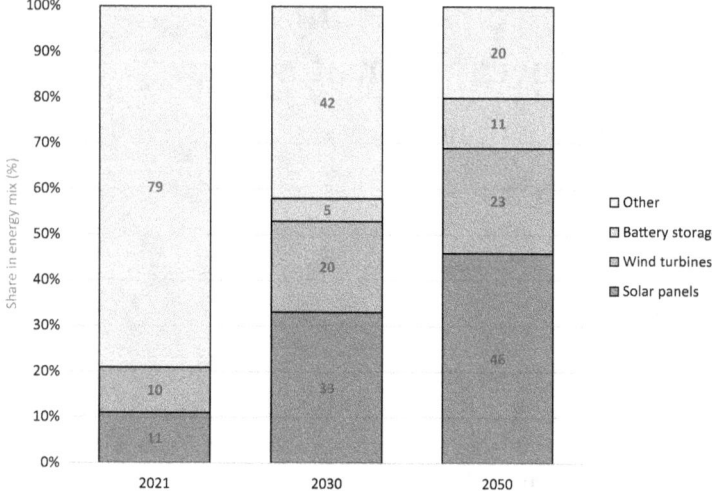

Figure 3.1 Change in energy mix toward the NZE Scenario. "Other" consists of renewables (hydro, bioenergy, solar thermal, and geothermal), nuclear, hydrogen, and ammonia, and fossil fuels with (from 2050) CO_2 capture and storage, or offset by direct CO_2 capture and storage from the air. The figures are from the International Energy Agency, 2021. Net Zero by 2050, A Roadmap for the Global Energy Sector. From bottom to top: solar panels, wind turbines, battery storage and others.

that as early as 2035, all new passenger cars and vans appearing on the European market should not emit CO_2 and NO_x. I estimate the number of new vehicles entering the global market in 2040 to be around 141 million, and I assume that all these new vehicles will be electric. To achieve this, 19% more electric vehicles will have to roll out of the assembly line each year starting in 2020. The question is whether the production capacity of the mines that provide the necessary raw materials for all these new electric cars can be scaled up fast enough. After 2040, the number of new electric cars entering the market each year will not have to increase as much. This makes the period between now and 2040 the most critical in terms of raw material supply.

China recognized and acted on the importance of a guaranteed supply of raw materials at least 15 years ago, entering into

The electric car and the energy transition: conflict or not? 43

cooperation agreements with countries where, in exchange for raw material contracts, it helps with such things as infrastructure construction. China also has raw materials of its own, such as rare earths. In 2020, an average of one battery factory a week was built in China.[1] Europe does not have many of the necessary raw materials and is far behind China in acquiring what it needs. In the past, the European Commission provided regular updates of a list of critical raw materials but took few concrete steps in ensuring their supply. That has now changed, triggered by the war in Ukraine.

> *To reduce the dependency of EU Member States on other countries for their raw materials, on March 16, 2023, the European Commission submitted a proposal to the European Parliament and the European Council for a new regulation to ensure a sustainable supply of critical raw materials.*[2] *This regulation was announced by Commission President Ursula Von Der Leyen as the Critical Raw Material Act. Its goal is to make Europe less dependent on supplies of critical raw materials from countries outside the European Union. The draft regulation names 34 critical raw materials, 16 of which are considered strategic. All major raw materials of electric cars belong to the group of strategic raw materials: cobalt, copper, lithium, manganese, natural graphite, nickel, and rare earths. The goal of the regulation is that, by 2030, the European Union should have (1) sufficient mining capacity to meet at least 10% of the need for strategic raw materials in finished products sold on the European market, if reserves are at least sufficient; (2) sufficient process capacity to meet 40% of the need for strategic raw materials in finished products sold on the European market (this refers to the process steps required to convert the raw material into intermediate products suitable for processing into a finished product); and (3) sufficient recycling capacity to meet 15% of the need for strategic raw materials in finished products sold on the European market.*

It will take some time, but it is certain that the demand for oil and gas, and thus the power of countries that export them, will diminish. The Middle East and Russia will lose power in this regard. Countries such as Chile, which has a lot of copper and lithium in its soil, the Democratic Republic of Congo, which has a large amount of cobalt and other resources, and Indonesia, which has a lot of nickel, will gain influence. The energy transition will therefore also change geopolitical relations. The war in Ukraine has highlighted how vulnerable the European Union is to the disruption of the supply of raw materials and products that we consider essential to our lifestyles: coal, oil, gas, certain metals, sunflower oil, and grain.

The material composition of electric vehicles is very different from that of fossil-fuel vehicles. Of the 15 metals that are much more prevalent in electric cars than in fossil-fuel cars, 14 are labeled critical by the European Commission:[3] aluminum, antimony, barium, boron, cobalt, copper, lithium, nickel, niobium, strontium, tantalum, vanadium, and the rare earth metals dysprosium and neodymium. I will explore which of these 14 metals are or will become most problematic for the timely realization of the energy transition.

Table 3.1 shows the expected distribution of these 14 metals in 2050 among electric cars, the rest of the energy transition, and all other applications. Here I have assumed that all new cars are electric from 2040 and that the International Energy Agency's NZE Scenario is followed. I have included two battery scenarios in the table for cobalt, copper, lithium, and nickel, because these are scenarios that are quite different from each other.

We see in Table 3.1 that the additional use of aluminum, antimony, barium, boron, niobium, strontium, tantalum, and vanadium due to the switch from fossil-fuel to electric cars will not interfere with the rest of the energy transition, either because they represent a relatively small proportion of total consumption, or because the metals are not used for the rest of the energy transition (i.e., strontium and tantalum). Furthermore, we see that the proportion of copper and lithium and of the rare earths dysprosium and neodymium needed for the energy transition is large, and that a significant proportion of these is earmarked for vehicle electrification. The share of cobalt and nickel depends on the battery scenario. Battery scenario B does not require any cobalt and nickel at all for vehicle electrification, while the share of cobalt and nickel required for vehicle electrification in battery scenario A is significant.

I therefore zoom in on cobalt, copper, dysprosium, lithium, neodymium, and nickel, as these six critical metals could pose problems due to lack of sufficient availability in the short term. For each of these six metals, Table 3.2 shows how high the annual increase in

Table 3.1 Estimated distribution of the use of 14 critical metals that are expected to be used much more in electric cars than in fossil-fuel cars in 2050

	Vehicle electrification	Rest of the energy transition	Other applications
Aluminum	3%	27%	69%
Antimony	8%	0%	92%
Barium	4%	0%	96%
Boron	0%	0%	100%
Cobalt			
Battery scenario A[a]	50%	27%	23%
Battery scenario B[b]	0%	53%	47%
Copper			
Battery scenario A	11%	59%	30%
Battery scenario B	13%	58%	30%
Dysprosium	31%	43%	26%
Lithium			
Battery scenario A	46%	39%	15%
Battery scenario B	30%	50%	20%
Neodymium	15%	52%	32%
Nickel			
Battery scenario A	40%	27%	32%
Battery scenario B	0%	46%	54%
Niobium	6%	0%	94%
Strontium	5%	0%	95%
Tantalum	14%	0%	86%
Vanadium	1%	97%	3%

Sources: International Energy Agency, 2021. Net Zero by 2050, A Roadmap for the Global Energy Sector; Henckens, M., 2022. The energy transition and energy equity: a compatible combination?. *Sustainability*, 14, 4781.

Notes: [a] Battery scenario A: Extrapolation of current average battery composition.
[b] Battery scenario B: 100% LFP batteries.

production must be to avoid shortages. Regarding the battery composition in electric cars, I have assumed the International Energy Agency's expectations for the battery mix in 2040;[4] in other words, battery scenario A in Table 3.1.

Table 3.2 Necessary production increase of six critical metals between 2020 and 2050 to ensure that all new cars in the world are electric from 2040, while not delaying the NZE Scenario (author's own calculations)

	Annual production increase between 1980 and 2020	Annual production increase between 2020 and 2050, necessary to achieve the goal of all new cars being electric by 2040 without compromising the achievement of the NZE Scenario as per the World Energy Outlook 2022
Cobalt	3.9%	9.0%
Copper	2.7%	6.2%
Dysprosium	6.1%	8.4%
Lithium	7.2%	12.4%
Neodymium	6.1%	7.7%
Nickel	3.0%	6.5%

Note: The growth rates in the left column are based on data from the U.S. Geological Survey, Mineral Commodity Summaries. Those in the right column are based on the battery mix projected by the International Energy Agency for 2040.

Table 3.3 Annual production increase of six metals between 2017 and 2022

	Annual production increase between 2017 and 2022 (%)
Cobalt	8.6
Copper	2.0
Dysprosium	15.4
Lithium	13.5
Neodymium	15.4
Nickel	8.5

As Table 3.2 shows, the production of all six metals have to be increased compared with growth rates over the past 40 years if all ambitions are to be met—growth rates that were already high.

Zooming in on production increases over the past five years (2017–2022; Table 3.3), we see that the required increase in production has clearly started for five of these six metals, with only copper lagging behind. This could be because copper recycling has improved over the same period.

Scaling up the production capacity does not therefore seem to have been a problem so far, except in the case of copper. The annual production increase for copper has been around 2% for some time, but will need to increase to 6%, or copper recycling will need to improve. These calculations do not take into account recycling of the six metals from the products and installations related to the energy transition (solar panels, wind turbines, power grids, batteries, and electric cars), because these products all have estimated lifespans of at least 20–30 years. As a result, the amount of recycled metal will not increase at nearly the same rate as the amount of "new" metal required for the energy transition in the period up to 2050.

If it is possible to sustain the annual increase in production of the last five years for cobalt, lithium, nickel, and the two rare earths until 2050, this will be enough to achieve the goal of all new cars being electric by 2040 for these metals without jeopardizing the realization of the NZE Scenario. Note that these production increases are huge. An annual production increase of 12.4% means that lithium production in 2050 must be as much as 33 times that of 2020. The supply of cobalt in 2050 will have to be 13 times that in 2020, and the annual production of nickel will have to be seven times greater. Finally, the annual production of rare earths will have to be 11 times higher in 2050 than in 2020. There is the escape route for nickel and cobalt of switching to an EV battery type without these metals, should availability problems arise. However, as far as I know, there are no alternative materials available as yet to replace lithium and the two rare earths.

Copper seems to be the problem child, given the discrepancy between the necessary production increase and the actual production increase. The necessary production increase of 6.2% per year implies that copper production in 2050 must be six times higher than in 2020. Incidentally, there is quite a bit of buffer capacity in the system for copper: the recycling rate of copper from products at the waste stage on a global scale is currently only about 45%, and a substantial increase in this is certainly possible. In richer countries, the recycling rate of copper from products at the waste stage is already 50–60%, and further improvement is certainly possible. As already mentioned, this is perhaps why the production of primary copper is not increasing as fast as the production of the other metals. Moreover, in its application as a conductor of electricity, copper can to some extent be substituted by aluminum, although this is not as good a conductor as copper.

Copper has already been partially replaced by aluminum in overhead high-voltage power transmission lines. It is, however, unclear to what extent copper is replaceable by aluminum in its application in electric motors, batteries, and inverters.

Whether the electric car can disrupt the rollout of the energy transition depends on whether the current rate of increase in the production of cobalt, lithium, nickel, and rare earths can be sustained long enough, and also on whether China and the Democratic Republic of Congo in particular will continue to supply the necessary raw materials to the world market in a timely and sufficient manner. An additional risk here is that Chinese companies have a significant share of cobalt mining in DR Congo, and that most of the processing of lithium and nickel ore to battery grade takes place in China.

Figure 3.2 shows that the transition from the fossil-fuel car to the electric car will take a significant toll on the use of resources that are also crucial to the energy transition. Note that Figure 3.2 does not include metal recycling from electric cars, wind turbines, solar panels, and stationary battery storage in the 2020–2050 period. The figures assume the battery mix expected by the International Energy Agency in 2040. If the development and introduction of cobalt- and nickel-free batteries accelerates, the shares of these two metals may decrease substantially compared with the percentages shown in Figure 3.2.

If resource supply were to become a bottleneck for the realization of the NZE Scenario, the production and installation of solar panels, wind turbines, power grids, and batteries may have to be prioritized over the production of electric vehicles at some point. After all, it would make no sense to manufacture electric cars using raw materials produced from fossil fuels and powered for a long time with electricity also generated by fossil fuels.

> *China temporarily reduced its rare earth exports in 2010. Following international protests and official complaints to the World Trade Organization, the restriction was lifted after four months. Nevertheless, the situation led to a six-fold increase in the price of rare earths in a short time.*
>
> *On July 5, 2023, the news broke that China would require special permits to export gallium and germanium—metals needed in chips—in response to export controls on advanced chip-making machines to China by Western countries.*

The electric car and the energy transition: conflict or not? 49

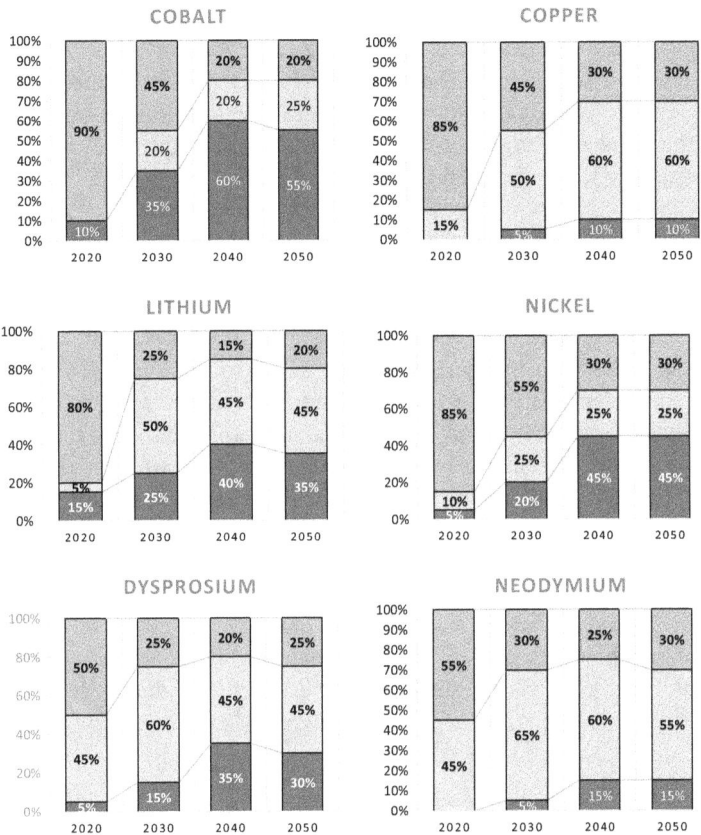

Figure 3.2 Change in the share of six metals in the transition to electric cars, the rest of the energy transition, and other applications between 2020 and 2050. I have assumed that all new cars are electric by 2040, that the NZE Scenario is realized, and that other uses of the metals continue to increase as they have over the past 40 years. Below: electric cars; middle: rest of the energy transition; above: other applications.

The International Energy Agency has calculated how many new mines and factories will be needed between 2021 and 2030 to produce EV batteries alone. The Agency based its calculations on the current average size of such mines and factories. For lithium, 30–50 additional mines are required, 40–60 additional mines are needed for nickel, and 11–17 additional mines are needed for cobalt. Furthermore, 29–50 cathode factories, 23–40 anode factories, and 52–90 battery cell factories are also needed.[5] The development and start-up of these new mines will take a long time: about 15 years on average. Building the required new factories is faster: from drawing board to starting production, this takes on average two to five years.[6]

The short-term supply of a commodity can become uncertain due to conflict between countries. Consider Russia's halt to the supply of gas and oil to European Union countries in 2022 due to the conflict between Russia and Ukraine, or China's temporary restriction on rare earth exports in 2010. The vulnerability of EU countries to the supply of a raw material is measured by the extent to which the European economy depends on the import of the raw material in question, as well as the extent to which the production and processing of that raw material are geographically concentrated in only a few countries outside the European Union. The quality of the administration of those countries is also an important factor. Administrative quality concerns aspects such as accountability, administrative transparency, political stability, the quality of regulations, implementation and enforcement, and the level of corruption. The major producing countries of cobalt, copper, lithium, nickel, and rare earths are listed in Table 3.4. For some materials, the concern is not so much the security of supply of the raw material but rather the supply of the corresponding battery-quality

Table 3.4 Production countries of critical metals in electric cars

Critical metal	Main producers in 2023 in order of production size[a]	Percentage of world production by named countries in 2023
Cobalt	Democratic Republic of Congo	74%
Copper	Chile, Peru, China, Democratic Republic of Congo	54%
Lithium	Australia, Chile, China	91%
Nickel	Indonesia, Philippines, Russia	62%
Rare earths	China	69%

Note: [a] U.S. Geological Survey, Mineral Commodity Summaries.

material. In this context, it is noteworthy that the planned new ore processing capacity of several critical metals is concentrated in only a few countries. For the 2023–2030 period, 49% of the new processing capacity of lithium ores is planned in China, 88% of nickel in Indonesia, and 36% of cobalt also in China (this information is derived from the Dutch newspaper *De Volkskrant*, July 31, 2023, and from data from the International Energy Agency).

The top three companies involved in the various stages of EV battery production are the following:[7]

- *Cathode production*: Sumitoma (Japan), Tianjin B&M Science and Technology (China), and Shenzhen Dynanonic (China). In 2021, these three companies accounted for about 25% of the global cathode production.
- *Anode production*: Ningbo Shanshan (China), BTR New Energy Materials (China), and Shanghai Putailai New Energy Technology (China). In 2021, these three companies accounted for 40% of the global anode production.
- *Battery production*: CATL (China), LG Energy Solution (Korea), and Panasonic (Japan). In 2021, these three companies represented about 70% of global battery production.
- *Electric car production*: Tesla (United States), VW Group (Germany), and BYD (China). In 2021, these three companies represented about 30% of global electric car production.

The conclusion of this chapter is that it is uncertain whether sufficient resources will always be available for the transition from fossil-fuel cars to electric cars without hindering the rest of the energy transition.

Notes

1 Sanderson, H., 2022. *Volt Rush: The Winners and Losers in the Race to Go Green*. Oneworld Publications, London.
2 European Commission, 2023. Proposal for a regulation of the European Parliament and of the Council establishing a framework for ensuring a secure and sustainable supply of critical raw materials and amending Regulations (EU)168/2013, (EU)2018/858, (EU)2018/1724 and (EU)2019/1020, COM(2023)160final 2023/0079(COD), March 16, 2023.
3 European Commission, 2023. Proposal for a regulation of the European Parliament and of the Council establishing a framework for ensuring a secure

and sustainable supply of critical raw materials and amending Regulations (EU)168/2013, (EU)2018/858, (EU)2018/1724 and (EU)2019/1020, COM(2023)160final 2023/0079(COD), March 16, 2023.
4 International Energy Agency, 2021. The Role of Critical Minerals in Clean Energy Transitions. www.iea.org/reports/the-role-of-critical-minerals-in-clean-energy-transitions
5 International Energy Agency, 2022. Global Supply Chains of EV Batteries. www.iea.org/reports/global-supply-chains-of-ev-batteries
6 International Energy Agency, 2022. Global Supply Chains of EV Batteries. www.iea.org/reports/global-supply-chains-of-ev-batteries
7 International Energy Agency, 2022. Global Supply Chains of EV Batteries. www.iea.org/reports/global-supply-chains-of-ev-batteries

4 Sensitivity analysis

The question I asked myself in the opening chapters of this book is how many electric cars the world can handle from a raw material availability perspective. To answer that question, I investigated whether the current European average vehicle ownership would also be possible and sustainable on a global scale, that is, for about ten billion people. My conclusion is that this is not the case, unless major progress is made quickly, lastingly, and globally in the recycling of the scarcest raw materials.

In this chapter, I examine the sensitivity of this outcome to the assumptions I made and the principles I used. I investigate two variants:

- What is the effect if the final average car ownership in the world does not stabilize at the level that I expect in the European Union in 2050—the fair scenario—but only at half of that? The answer to this question is the same as the answer to the question of what the effect would be if car engineers managed to halve the amount of mineral raw materials per electric car compared to the current average raw material use.
- What is the effect if the recoverable amount of raw materials turns out to be two-thirds lower than the optimistic amount I assumed?

Question 1: What is the effect of halving the—assumed—final number of vehicles and/or halving the use of raw materials per vehicle?

Currently, average car ownership in the world is about 3.5 times lower than that in Europe, at 18 cars per 100 inhabitants worldwide

DOI: 10.4324/9781003509431-4

54 Sensitivity analysis

versus 60 cars per 100 inhabitants in the European Union. These are averages. In Bangladesh, car ownership is currently about three cars per 100 inhabitants and in the United States, it is about 84 cars per 100 inhabitants.

In the previous chapters, I examined what happens if the average world vehicle ownership increases to the current European level and stabilizes at 68 vehicles per 100 inhabitants. This includes buses, vans, and trucks. I called this the fair scenario.

If the average world car ownership were to rise above the current European average, this would be even less sustainable than the fair scenario from a raw material availability perspective. I will therefore not discuss the raw material effects of such a scenario.

I have investigated how my conclusions change if I assume that the final number of vehicles in the world stabilizes at half the number I assumed for the fair scenario, namely 34 vehicles per 100 inhabitants, or if the use of resources per vehicle could be reduced by half. Of course, halving the raw material use for vehicles can also be achieved through a combination of limiting car ownership and a lower raw material content per car.

I only consider the scarcest raw materials that are used in electric cars and only those whose use in electric cars is substantial compared to their use in other applications. This means that, in this context, I only consider antimony, copper, molybdenum, and nickel. The results of my analysis are shown in Table 4.1. For nickel, the outcome is very dependent on the battery scenario. Nickel in battery scenarios 4 and 5 is not included in the table, because in those scenarios the nickel use

Table 4.1 Decrease in annual resource use compared to resource use if the fair scenario were realized (rounded to 5%)

	Effect of halving the number of electric cars, or halving the use of raw materials in electric cars, on the total annual use of raw materials compared to the annual use of raw materials when realizing the full fair scenario
Antimony	−5%
Copper, all battery scenarios	−10%
Molybdenum	−5%
Nickel, battery scenarios 1 and 2	−15%

in electric cars is very small compared to other applications of nickel. Hence, in battery scenarios 4 and 5, the demand that electric cars place on the available amount of nickel is not sensitive to halving the number of vehicles. The nickel consumption in nickel battery scenario 3 is lower than that in battery scenarios 1 and 2; therefore, I have only included battery scenarios 1 and 2 in the table for nickel.

The table shows that halving the number of electric cars compared to the number assumed in the fair scenario leads to a decrease in the annual demand of raw materials between 5% and 15%, depending on the raw material. This decrease is not that large. This is because most applications of antimony, copper, molybdenum, and nickel are not in electric cars.

Assuming the high estimate of the raw material supply, copper will be exhausted only a few years later (< five years) than in the fair scenario. The effect is somewhat larger for nickel. Halving the number of electric vehicles or raw material use compared with that assumed for the fair scenario results in an extension of nickel availability by approximately 75 years, at least if I assume the battery scenarios with the highest nickel use. In the battery scenarios without nickel, halving the number of vehicles obviously has little effect on the depletion rate of nickel, because there is only a limited amount of nickel in the rest of the car. For antimony and molybdenum, the postponement of the moment of depletion due to halving the number of electric cars or the use of raw materials is even less than for copper, and therefore small.

The conclusion is that depletion of scarce raw materials is a problem caused by the combination of all applications of those raw materials, to which electric cars make a limited contribution. Efforts to reduce raw material consumption by electric cars alone are of little use if simultaneous efforts are not made on all fronts to increase the recycling rate and replacement of scarce raw materials.

I point out that limiting car ownership in the world to twice its current level would, in a fair world, mean that the average car ownership in the richest part of the world halves, while in the poorest parts of the world it rises significantly. This will require robust measures in prosperous countries, which will probably only be acceptable to the population if good mobility alternatives are developed in a timely and ample manner, to limit the impact on perceived prosperity. The only alternatives to avoid these types of difficult measures are greatly increasing the recycling of raw materials and/or accepting continued inequality in the world.

56 Sensitivity analysis

Question 2: What is the effect if the amount of raw materials is only a third of what I assumed?

Apart from gold, most raw materials are not mined deeper than one kilometer below the Earth's surface. In the first chapters of this book, my optimistic starting point was that in the future it will become profitable to extract all raw materials up to a depth of three kilometers below the Earth's surface. Suppose this assumption is too optimistic and that the available quantity of raw materials is two-thirds less than I assumed. I have calculated the effect of this, and the results are shown in Figure 4.1.

We see in the figure that, assuming the high estimate of the raw material supply, only copper will be depleted in around 2120 and the other five metals will remain available for 50 years to even almost 300 years (nickel). On the other hand, if the raw material supply turns out to be only one-third of the high estimate I originally assumed,

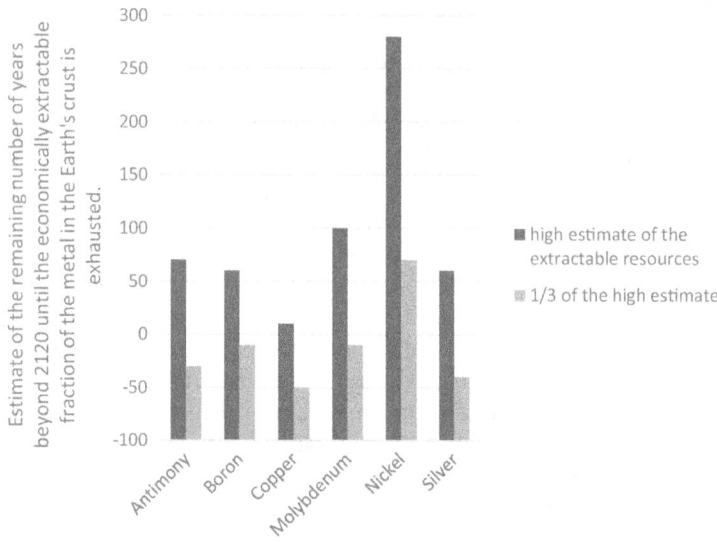

Figure 4.1 Estimate of the remaining number of years beyond 2120 until the economically recoverable fraction of six scarce metals is exhausted. The assumption is that the recycling rate will not increase compared to 2020 and that economic growth, and thus the increase in the use of the six metals, will continue to increase at the same rate as between 1980 and 2015.

Sensitivity analysis 57

then all metals in Figure 4.1, except nickel, will be depleted before 2120. The time at which five of the six scarcest raw materials are then expected to be depleted is on average about half a century to a century sooner, and for nickel even two centuries.

So, at one-third of the optimistic raw material supply, the fair scenario will not be feasible at all in 2120 as far as electric cars are concerned, unless

- the recycling rate of the scarcest raw materials is drastically increased and/or
- the scarcest raw materials are replaced by less scarce raw materials.

As we saw in the answer to Question 1, limiting car ownership alone will not contribute much to postponing the depletion of the metals discussed. This therefore only makes sense in combination with far-reaching savings measures across a broad front.

The uncertainty in the depletion periods of the scarcest raw materials should make it necessary to err on the side of caution. I think it is risky and unethical to mortgage the future by speculating that the development of technology together with the mechanism of the free market will lead to a solution, just as has always happened in the past when faced with scarcity. We must realize that future generations will enjoy the benefits or suffer the consequences of the steps that the current generation does or does not take to conserve resources.

5 Five critical metals in electric cars

Barring a major disaster, the global vehicle fleet will not only be electrified but will continue to grow in the coming decades. This will require many additional raw materials. Some of these are geologically scarce, and for some it is questionable whether their production can be scaled up fast enough. It became clear in Chapter 3 that the massive and rapid conversion from fuel cars to electric cars could get in the way of a smooth energy transition if the production capacity of cobalt, copper, lithium, nickel, and rare earths cannot be scaled up quickly enough, or if production countries implement production or export restrictions for one reason or another. On top of that, depletion is imminent in the longer term for some metals used in electric cars.

In this chapter, I take a closer look at the metals that may pose short- and/or long-term availability problems. What uses do they have beyond electric cars? Which companies and countries are involved in their production? Where are the main remaining reserves? What possibilities exist for substitution and recycling?

Copper: aorta of the energy transition

In 2007, Auguste Rodin's famous statue *The Thinker* was stolen from the garden of the Singer Museum in Laren in the Netherlands, along with six other statues. Most were made of bronze, an alloy of copper and tin. The police therefore suspected that the thieves were interested in the copper, not the artistic value of the statues but "the simple price per kilo", as a police spokesman told the Dutch newspaper *NRC Handelsblad*.[1]

Five critical metals in electric cars 59

Rodin's sculpture was recovered two days after the theft, badly damaged but intact. The museum was lucky, because stolen statues are usually cut into pieces and resold unrecognizable to a scrap dealer, eventually ending up in a smelter to be reused as secondary copper. Secondary copper is copper that is recovered from a copper-containing product, while primary copper comes directly from a copper mine.

It is no coincidence that thieves are targeting copper. This semi-precious metal has been hunted for years; not only in bronze statues, but also in power lines and signal and switch cables along railroad tracks. In early June 2023, half of the cables in a solar park in Deurne, the Netherlands, were stolen, containing a total of 5,000 kilograms of copper. The damage: €500,000 according to the owner.[2] Copper is worth a lot more than metals such as aluminum and iron. The kilogram price averaged $7.76 in the third quarter of 2022—much higher than that of aluminum ($2.23) or iron ($0.17). Because of the higher specific gravity, the price difference per unit volume is even higher: one liter of copper costs about $70, compared to $6.40 for the same volume of aluminum, and $1.30 for one liter of iron.

This makes copper attractive to thieves, although not as attractive as the more expensive nickel, tin, and cobalt, or the much more expensive gold and silver. However, these metals are generally much harder to steal: they usually occur only in small quantities in a product, and gold and silver certainly are much better secured.

It would not be surprising if copper were even more expensive, as the demand for copper in modern society is insatiable. A wind turbine—5,000 kilograms of copper; an average house—100 kilograms. The outdoor unit of a heat pump—two kilograms. A laptop computer—100 grams; and a cell phone—10 grams (which may not seem much, until you realize that about five million phones are sold every day worldwide). An average electric car requires about 120 kilograms of copper, which is used in the battery, the motor, and about 1.5 kilometers of copper wiring.[3]

First and foremost, the energy transition means that everything that was previously done using fossil fuels must now be done with sustainably generated electricity. In a 2014 article in the journal *Science*, the science journalist Richard Kerr called electrons "the lifeblood" of the modern economy, with the blood vessels made of copper.[4] Therefore, replacing coal, oil, and gas with clean energy can only succeed if there is enough copper available worldwide.

> There is evidence that copper was used by humans more than 10,000 years ago due to its special properties, for example in figurines and coins. However, copper was only used on a larger scale from the beginning of the Bronze Age (which followed the Stone Age): from about 3300 BC to 1,200 BC. These periods are named after the main material that was used for tools and weapons. Bronze is an alloy of copper and tin, with the tin content varying between 10% and 30%. The addition of tin makes bronze harder and less ductile than copper. Bronze also has a lower melting point than copper, making it easier to cast objects from. After 1200 BC, people mastered the art of making carbon steel, and weapons were increasingly made of steel since iron was much more widely available and therefore cheaper. Steel is also stronger and lighter than bronze, which is a major advantage in weapons.

The fact that copper is so important has to do with its properties. Copper is highly corrosion resistant—which is also why it is called a semi-precious metal. It is also relatively easy to work and is used in alloys such as brass (copper/zinc), bronze (copper/tin), and copper/nickel alloys, which further increases its applicability.

What makes copper crucial to the energy transition is that it is an excellent conductor of electricity. It is a key component of alternators, electric motors, and batteries and is widely used to transport electricity. Inverters, which sit between a power source and an electrical device to ensure that the power supplied is of the right quality, cannot be designed without copper.

In 2018, 45% of all copper was used in cables for the transmission and distribution of electricity, but copper is also used in water pipes, appliances for heating and cooling, and communication lines. Electrical appliances, in industry and at home, accounted for 14% of copper use in 2018, 13% was for the transport sector (8% in electric cars, 1% in non-electric cars, and the rest in railroads and ships), and furthermore copper is used in a wide array of applications such as fluid valves, fittings, tools, electronics, ammunition, and coins (together 29%).[5]

Because copper is such a convenient and versatile metal, its production has increased tremendously over the past century, from

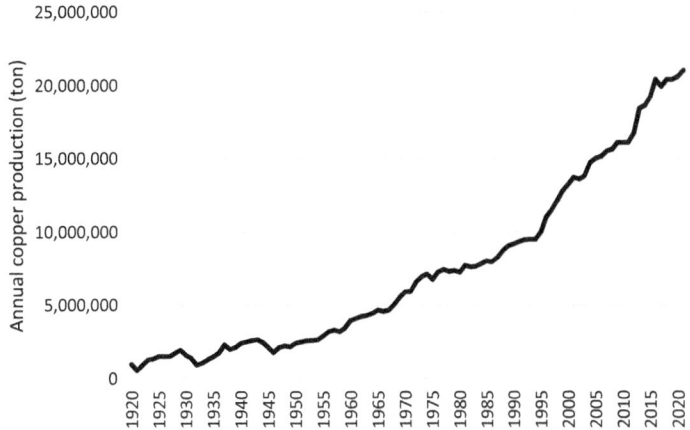

Figure 5.1 World copper production between 1920 and 2023.

Source: U.S. Geological Survey, Copper Statistics, Last Modification, May 3, 2021 and Mineral Commodity Summary, January 2024.

about 1 million tons per year in 1920 to 21 million tons in 2021. See Figure 5.1. Of all the copper humanity has ever used, 70% has been mined in the past 70 years and 50% in the past 25 years. Since 1965, annual copper production has doubled every 25 years, representing an annual increase of 2.8% or a quadrupling in the 50 years since 1965. If we continue producing copper at this rate, in 2100, its production will be 11 times higher than in 2018. This figure will probably be somewhat lower, however, as copper will undoubtedly be recovered from end-of-life products on a larger scale than today.

In poorer countries, the increase in copper demand is directly related to the increase in gross national product. China, for example, has become a huge importer of copper in recent decades. While in 1995 the country accounted for about 10% of world copper consumption, by 2014, it accounted for about 50%.[6] China is not the only country where demand for copper has risen sharply, a similar trend can be observed in India, Brazil, and other emerging economies. The infrastructure in these countries is being expanded, many new buildings are being constructed, requiring proportionately large amounts of copper, and the general level of prosperity of the population is rising, all leading to an increase in copper demand. The demand for copper in richer countries is increasing less rapidly than the gross national product for the same reasons, as much of the infrastructure is more or less well developed.

Surprisingly, increasing demand for copper has barely led to an increase in its price, which has hovered for nearly a century between roughly $3 and $8 per kilogram[7] (expressed in 2021-dollar value[8]). This is all the more remarkable because copper ore concentrations are decreasing and so more must be mined for the same amount of metal. On the one hand, technological improvements have so far managed to offset this cost-increasing effect. On the other hand, the market apparently does not yet consider the geological scarcity of copper, which is really looming on the horizon, to be a price-determining factor.[9]

Geological scarcity does not mean that all the copper in the Earth's crust is in danger of disappearing. This is unlikely to happen. Depletion is about the cost of extracting copper becoming so high that at some point it is no longer economically viable to do so. The copper is then so deep, or only available in such low concentrations, that mining it becomes pointless. It is difficult to say when this moment will be reached, as it also depends on technological developments. There are, however, limits to these scenarios.

The average copper concentration in the Earth's crust is 50 parts per million, or 0.005%. That seems little, but it means that the top kilometer of the Earth's continental crust contains about 20,000 billion tons of copper. That amount, as mentioned, is far from being extractable, as only where there are "enriched" copper deposits is it economically interesting to extract copper.

The concentration of copper in mined ore has decreased significantly: from 10% to –20% in the nineteenth century (i.e., every ton of ore contained 100–200 kilograms of copper), to 2–3% in the first half of the twentieth century, and less than 1% today. Even copper concentrations between 0.4% and 0.8% are now of interest to mining companies.[10] At the current rate of extraction increase, the copper percentage in copper ore may have dropped to 0.1% by the end of the twenty-second century.[11]

This figure, 0.1%, is still a factor of 20 higher than the average concentration of copper in the Earth's crust. There are two reasons why copper extraction from general rock costs disproportionately more energy than the extraction of copper from copper ore. Not only is the concentration of copper in rock much lower than in copper ore, but the copper in it is also often chemically bound in a different, stronger way than in copper ore. This means that it takes 100 to 1,000 times more energy to release that copper.[12] Extracting just one kilogram of copper from rock would cost an amount of energy equal to the amount used by a family with an electricity consumption of 4,500 kWh per year over a 20-year period.[13] With 100 kilograms of copper in the home, that would represent an energy bill of 2,000 years, which is of course unthinkable.

About 85% of all the copper ever extracted from the ground is present in products still in use. This is estimated at 600 million tons worldwide, or an average of 80 kilograms per person.

The total amount of extractable copper is estimated at between five and six billion tons.[14] Most of this resides in the upper kilometer of the Earth's crust. Of this, 3.5 billion tons have not yet been "officially" discovered, but estimated based on the geology in different areas of the world. See Figure 5.2. If we assume—very optimistically, as will be shown later—that it will be technologically and economically

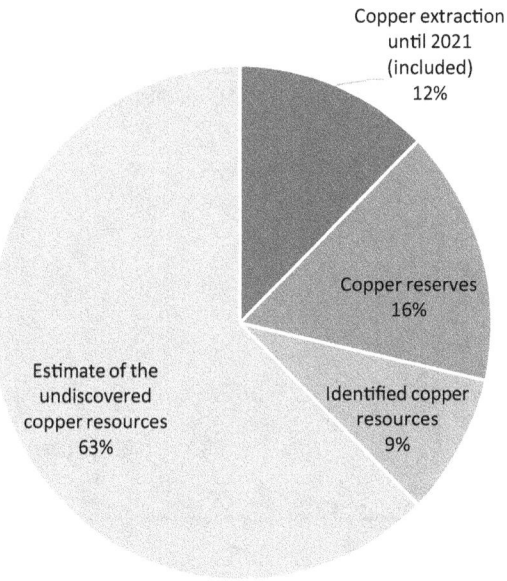

Figure 5.2 Already mined copper and copper in the ground. Data from the U.S. Geological Survey.

Source: U.S. Geological Survey, 2018, Assessment of undiscovered copper resources of the world, 2015, Scientific Investigations Report 2018-5160, Version 12, December 2021.

possible in the future to extract all the copper in enriched copper deposits up to three kilometers deep in the Earth's crust, the total yet undiscovered copper could rise to about 10 billion tons.

There is also a quantity of copper on the ocean floor in deep-sea nodules (roughly 0.7 billion tons) and in submarine massive sulfides (estimated at about 0.03 billion tons). The quantities are not entirely negligible, but they are not very large compared to the extractable copper in the continental Earth's crust. The responsible exploitation of these deep-sea resources is challenging from the point of view of environmental protection, although whether the world will care very much is questionable. Various companies have been stepping up the pressure to obtain a permit for deep-sea mining, or at least to explore its possibilities, in recent years.

Most of the known copper supply—about half—is in the Americas, in particular South America. See Figure 5.3. Chile has traditionally been the world's leading copper producer,[15] accounting for 27% of world copper production in 2021. Copper is also widely mined in its northern neighbor Peru. Together with China, DR Congo, the United States, and Australia, these countries accounted for 65% of world copper production in 2021. European countries, with the exception of Poland, produce hardly any copper at all, and are unlikely to do so in the future.

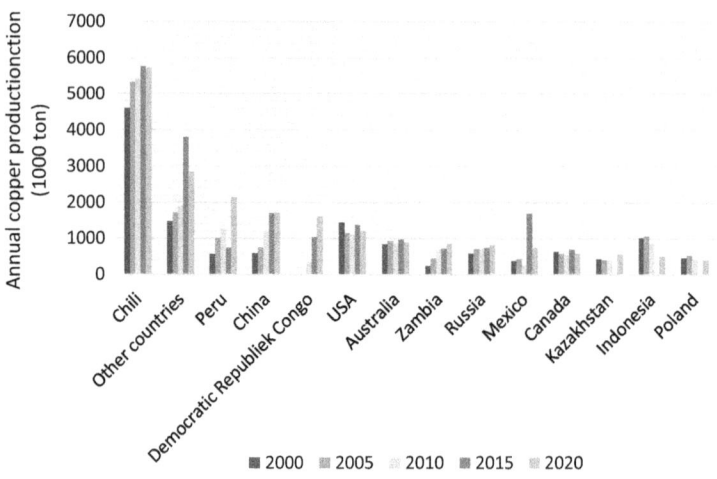

Figure 5.3 The 13 major copper-producing countries from 2000 to 2020.

China is far less dominant in copper production than in several other metals and is likely to remain a net importer of copper in the future. China's massive copper consumption, currently about half of global consumption, can by no means be covered by domestic production. As a result, Chinese companies are also active in copper mining in Chile, and particularly in DR Congo.

Copper ore is mostly mined in open-pit mines, so above ground. Such copper mines are actually giant craters in the landscape, such as at Chuquicamata in Chile. This is the largest copper mine in the world, where copper has been mined since 1915. The crater has a length of five kilometers, a width of three kilometers, and a depth of one kilometer. In 2019, the mine was expanded with underground shafts. The impact on water, soil, and air in the area is considerable. Each kilogram of copper produces 100–200 times more waste, and water consumption is enormous. Large quantities of water are needed to process ore and to cool machinery, and to sometimes prevent the dust clouds created following the explosions used to loosen the ore. The water in the Chuquicamata area has become severely polluted over the years, and only in the past few years have environmental permits been tightened, although their enforcement is not without problems.

The copper industry

Codelco is a Chilean state-owned company that limits its operations to Chile. It extracts about 30% of the copper in Chile, accounting for over 8% of world production. The eight non-Chilean companies in the list are private companies that operate in several countries. The ten companies in the list together produce about 45% of all the world's primary copper. All the companies listed produce a range of other commodities besides copper.

Copper mining in Russia, Kazakhstan, and China is carried out entirely by state-owned companies. Chinese companies are also active in copper mining in Peru and DR Congo, as well as in China.

Table 5.1 The ten largest copper mining companies in 2020 (numbers rounded to 0.5%)

Company	Country	Share of world copper production in 2020 (%)	Copper-mined geographies
Codelco	Chile	8.5	Chile
BHP	Australia	6.0	Chile, Peru, Australia
Glencore	Switzerland	6.0	Chile, Peru, DR Congo, Zambia, Canada
Freeport-McMoRan	USA	5.5	Chile, Peru, USA, Indonesia
Southern Copper Corporation	Mexico	5.0	Peru, Mexico
First Quantum Minerals	Canada	3.5	DR Congo, Zambia, Canada
KGHM Polska Miedz	Poland	2.5	Chile, USA, Poland
Antofagasta	Chile	2.5	Chile
Rio Tinto	UK	2.5	Chile, Peru, Australia
Anglo American plc	UK	2.5	Chile, Peru

Information from Evanoff, M., 2022. Top 10 Biggest Copper Mining Companies—Codelco, BHP, Glencore, and more, https://miningfeeds.com/top-10-biggest-copper-mining-companies-codelco-bhp-glencore-and-more, *August 6, 2022.*

Land degradation is also one of the consequences of copper mining. The ground is cracked open to release the ore, and sometimes entire slopes are removed. Soil erosion, landslides, and other damage result. In Chuquicamata, this has led to the disturbance of natural habitats and local ecosystems and biodiversity loss.

The biggest problem with copper mining is energy consumption. Extraction is a complex, energy-guzzling, mechanical-chemical-thermal process, and the amount of energy required increases as the copper concentration in the ore decreases and deeper mining is required. Roughly speaking, a halving of the copper concentration in the copper ore is associated with a doubling of the energy required to produce copper. It is expected that the amount of energy required to extract a kilogram of copper will have tripled at least by 2050 and may increase tenfold by 2100 compared to today.[16]

Thus, as the demand for copper grows, more and more energy will be needed for copper extraction—which only further increases the demand for copper. The gradual depletion of higher ore grades is characteristic of all mineral resources. It is therefore not necessarily the amount of a mineral in the Earth's crust that leads to scarcity, but the effort required to extract it in terms of energy use, water use, waste production, and landscape degradation.

It makes a big difference whether copper is mined at a depth of one or three kilometers. The average temperature in the Earth's crust at a depth of three kilometers below sea level is about 90 °C,[17] which makes mining at that depth extremely difficult and very costly. Conditions for miners are particularly harsh, and the water used has to be constantly cooled. It is obvious that such conditions call for largely robotic mines.

Currently, although there are some mines with shafts up to four kilometers below ground level (and 2.5 kilometers below sea level), these are gold mines, which must be cooled with ice slurry to keep the working temperature bearable. This is affordable only because gold yields about 5,000 times more per kilogram than copper.

Copper mining at a depth greater than three kilometers is therefore unlikely to happen, and so the undiscovered copper deposits will not exceed by much the 3.5 billion tons calculated by the U.S. Geological Survey.[18] Given the rate of increase in demand for copper, this means that copper could be depleted in about a century.[19] The process of depletion can be slowed if more copper is recovered from end-of-life products. This may seem obvious, but in practice, much used copper is still lost unnecessarily in landfills and waste incinerators. Worldwide, only about 45% of all copper in discarded items is recycled, while just over half of used copper (51%) ends up in landfills.[20] The more copper is recycled, the longer it will take for copper to be depleted. In theory, the depletion of copper could be pushed forward by centuries in this way, providing that copper recycling is ramped up in a timely and sufficient manner (see Table 5.2).

Not all used copper can be recycled. Some will always disappear, whether through food, through the use of copper-containing chemicals (wood preservatives, fungicides, pigments, antifouling paint for ships), or through the corrosion of copper-containing objects. Humans require

Table 5.2 Relationship between copper depletion and recycling

Copper recycling	Depletion after 2020 (in years)
45% (now)	90
60% from 2100	110
70% from 2100	140
80% from 2100	190
90% from 2100	330

Note: The assumptions are the total amount of extractable copper is five billion tons, the fair scenario is completed in 2100, and recycling of copper gradually increases from 45% today to the indicated percentage in 2100.

1.5–3 milligrams of copper per day in their food, and animals and plants also need copper: pigs, for example, require about 12 milligrams per kilogram of feed. Of course, copper re-enters nature through the feces of humans and animals. In total, the non-recyclable part of copper accounts for about 2% of annual copper consumption.[21]

Recycling companies that recover copper do so as carefully as possible, mainly because of the relatively high price of the metal, but also because steel and aluminum mills prefer not to have copper in the scrap metal that they supply. Even so, it is almost inevitable that some copper is left behind and "lost" in the steel and aluminum cycles. This is called *downcycling*. The amount of copper unintentionally entering the steel and aluminum cycles in this way is currently estimated at 4% of annual copper consumption.[22]

As a conductor of electric current, copper can in theory be replaced by aluminum. Although copper is clearly superior to aluminum in terms of electrical conductivity, it has already been replaced by aluminum in several applications, such as the transmission of electric current over long distances by means of high-voltage power lines. The aluminum high-voltage power lines may be much thicker than the copper ones, but that is not a problem because aluminum is much lighter than copper. Copper is still used in the distribution of electricity in cities and towns and for power lines in the home, although here too it may be replaced by aluminum in the future. It is conceivable that copper windings in electric motors and alternators could also be replaced by aluminum windings, although the efficiency will then decrease. Working safely with aluminum wiring is more complicated than with copper, because aluminum expands more, and because aluminum oxide is a poor conductor of electricity. These issues can

Five critical metals in electric cars   69

lead to bad electrical contact and overheating if the installation is not done properly. Moreover, it takes three times more energy to extract aluminum from bauxite than copper from copper ore. Aluminum is, however, much less scarce than copper, and so replacing copper with aluminum would, in theory, counteract copper depletion. Nevertheless, much more practical experience will have to be gained before copper can be replaced by aluminum in all its applications.

Lithium lakes

The name lithium is derived from the Greek *lithos*, meaning "stone." It was discovered by the Swede Johan Arfwedson in 1817 while he was examining minerals from the Utö mines. A bar of pure lithium looks like a bar of aluminum but is lighter and softer. You can easily cut a bar of lithium metal with a knife. Lithium is also highly reactive, unlike pure aluminum. Lithium metal therefore needs to be stored in oil; otherwise it will react with oxygen and water in the air. If you place a little bar of lithium in a glass of water, not only will it float because it is half as light as water, but it will begin to dance on the surface as it reacts violently with the water. After a short time, lithium would have completely dissolved in the water, which would have become boiling hot. The gas produced in the reaction between lithium and water is flammable hydrogen, a reaction that is even used to power torpedoes.

This spectacular behavior shows why lithium does not occur as such in nature; it is far too reactive for that. Lithium is always found in lithium salts, for example as lithium chloride. Like table salt (sodium chloride), lithium salts are mostly extracted from salt lakes or underground salt deposits. Another source of lithium is lithium-bearing stony minerals, such as pegmatite.[i][23] Lithium is the lightest metal there is, and a liter of lithium weighs only a little more than half a kilogram. The fact that lithium is so light is an advantage for its application in batteries.

We could regard lithium as the petroleum of the twenty-first century. Electric cars run on rechargeable lithium-ion batteries, and when the sun shines in abundance and the wind is blowing, large stationary lithium-ion batteries can temporarily store the surplus electricity generated and discharge it again when there is no sun and wind. Oil can only be burned once, producing CO_2, but lithium ions

---

i   Lithium is distributed among the different sources as follows: lithium in salt deposits, 58%; in pegmatite, 26%; in lithium-containing clays, 7%; in oilfield brine, 3%; in geothermal brines, 3%; and in jadarite, 3%

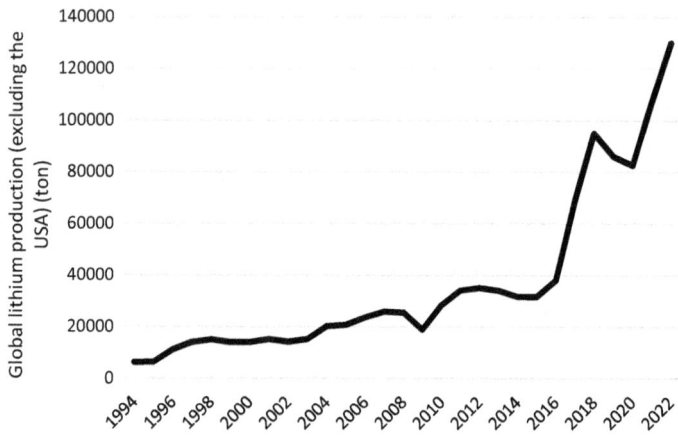

Figure 5.4 World lithium production expressed in tons of lithium from 1994 to 2023.

in a rechargeable lithium-ion battery are used repeatedly, almost like a miracle oil. Virtually all rechargeable devices feature lithium-ion batteries. Although the main application of lithium is in lithium-ion batteries, it also has many other applications. Until recently, its main application was as lithium oxide in glass and ceramics, where it lowers the melting point and viscosity of glass, making it easier to process. Lithium metal is also used in alloys with aluminum and magnesium to make these metals stronger and lighter. Lithium chloride is used as hygroscopic material. Lithium stearate is used in lubricants, and lithium carbonate is the active ingredient in pills for the suppression of bipolar disorder and has been used as such since 1949. Lithium hydride is used in the storage of hydrogen. However, all of these applications have been completely outstripped in recent years by the use of lithium in lithium-ion and lithium batteries.[ii] In 2010, 14% of lithium was used for batteries; by 2018, this had risen to 57%, and by 2022 to 80%.[24] Everyone knows that lithium-ion batteries are used in smartphones, laptops, and rechargeable hand tools, but the really important application of lithium is in lithium-ion EV batteries, an application that will undoubtedly continue to grow in importance as fuel cars are replaced by electric cars.

---

ii Lithium-ion batteries are rechargeable, but lithium batteries are not.

Five critical metals in electric cars 71

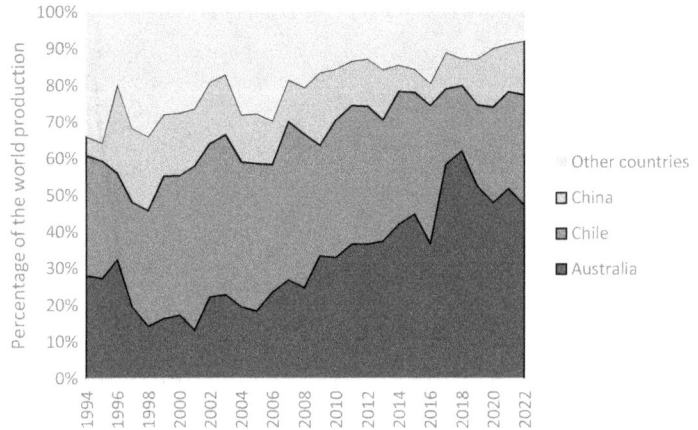

Figure 5.5 Major lithium-producing countries between 1994 and 2022. The main "other countries" are, in order of production in 2022: Argentina (5%), Brazil (2%), Zimbabwe (1%), Portugal (0.5%), and Canada (0.4%). The production of lithium in the United States is not provided by the U.S. Geological Survey, but I estimate it at several thousand tons per year, or a few percent of world production, so in the same range as Argentina and Brazil.

The global production of lithium was 6,100 tons in 1994, increasing to 130,000 tons by 2022—more than 20 times as much in 28 years (see Figure 5.4). Lithium production rose particularly sharply after 2016, corresponding to the breakthrough of the electric car and lithium-ion batteries in rechargeable devices.

The United States was the largest producer of lithium for most of the twentieth century, but this has changed profoundly. By 2022, the world's two main lithium-producing countries were Australia and Chile, accounting for 47% and 30% of world production, respectively. In Australia, lithium is extracted mainly from pegmatite mines, and in Chile from brine (see Figure 5.5).

China is the world's third largest lithium producer, with 15% of world production in 2022. China is dominant in processing lithium into materials suitable as raw materials for rechargeable batteries, for example lithium carbonate, lithium chloride, or lithium hydroxide. Several countries export lithium ore to China for processing into a pure lithium compound suitable for use in batteries. Increasingly,

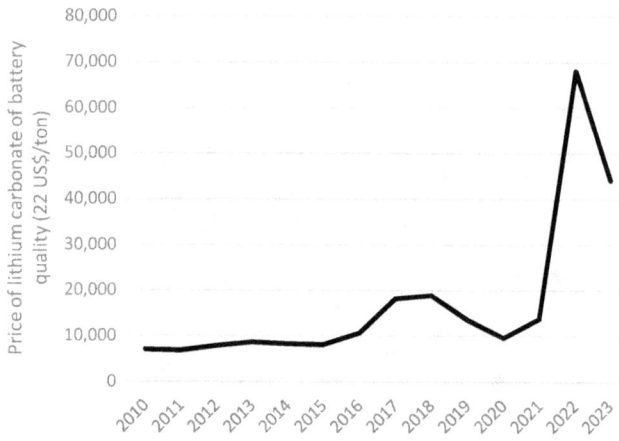

Figure 5.6 Price development of lithium carbonate (battery grade) between 2010 and 2023, expressed in $22 per ton.

Source: U.S. Geological Survey, 2023. Mineral Commodity Summaries, Lithium.

Chinese companies are setting up lithium refining plants or even battery plants in other countries where lithium is mined, such as Argentina, Zimbabwe, and Bolivia. This stems in part from the understandable desire of these countries to share in the value-added from lithium when it is processed from ore to battery raw material and then to batteries. In 2020, China controlled 70–80% of the world's lithium refining, 75–80% of lithium-ion battery cell production, and 60% of the world's lithium-ion battery production.[25]

After a rather long period without much real growth, the lithium price increased considerably from 2016, coinciding with the strong increase in its demand. By 2022, lithium prices rose to almost $70,000 per ton of battery-grade lithium carbonate (see Figure 5.6). But, in 2023, they fell again substantially. Reasons include the slumping market for new electric cars in China and the rapid global growth in lithium production.

EV traction batteries contain between five and ten kilograms of lithium on average, depending on the battery capacity. Lithium production will need to increase by about 12% annually up to 2050 to achieve the International Energy Agency's NEZ Scenario and the goal of all new cars in the world being electric from 2040. This means that lithium production will need to continue to rise, from 130 kilotons of lithium in 2022 to about 3,500 kilotons in 2050, an increase of a factor of 27

Five critical metals in electric cars 73

in less than 30 years. As the actual increase in lithium production was 13.5% per year in the five years between 2017 and 2022, it does seem possible to scale up lithium production fast enough. The share of lithium demand for electric cars is expected to increase from 15% in 2020 to 35–40% in 2050. The rest of the energy transition will account for about 45% of lithium demand in 2050, mainly for stationary electric batteries. The remainder of lithium use in 2050 (15–20%) will be for the other lithium applications identified at the beginning of this section.

The increase in demand for lithium will certainly not remain as high as it is today, because lithium will increasingly be recovered from end-of-life batteries, and because the increase in the number of cars in the world will gradually level off and stabilize. Currently (2023), lithium is hardly recovered from end-of-life batteries,[26] as the emphasis is on the recovery of more precious metals such as cobalt, nickel, copper, and aluminum. However, this will change. In the European Commission's draft Critical Raw Materials Act, lithium for batteries has been labeled a strategic raw material, meaning that the European Union's goal is for at least 15% of the lithium in new lithium-ion batteries to consist of recovered lithium by 2030. The European Battery Regulation states that at least 50% of lithium from batteries must be recovered by the end of 2027, and at least 80% by the end of 2032.

Because of its application in batteries, lithium is often named as a raw material that could become scarce. As researchers from Leuven wrote in a report for the European non-ferrous metals industry association Eurometaux:

> Europe currently imports most of its lithium-ion batteries, used in electric vehicles and grid storage. Today less than 3% of battery production happens in Europe. China, Korea, and Japan account for more than 90% of worldwide production. The European Commission aims to fully cover its needs through domestic batteries production from 2025.[27]

This seems rather ambitious. In an interview with the Dutch newspaper *NRC*, an example is given by Henry Sanderson, author of *Volt Rush: The Winners and Losers in the Race to Go Green* and currently working at an agency researching the raw material chain for lithium batteries:

> [China's] success is partly the result of Western indifference. Ten years ago, for example, a Chinese company was able to buy

Australia's largest lithium mine, the lithium mine with the lowest production costs in the world. Australian politicians allowed that at the time. No one was paying attention then.

The rapidly increasing demand for lithium is leading to an intensified search, and so new lithium discoveries. On March 7, 2023, the Dutch newspaper *De Volkskrant* reported the discovery of a large new deposit of lithium in Iran, said to be the second largest deposit in the world, at 8.5 million tons. The exploitation of new lithium mines is also being planned in many other countries. In Europe, for example, preparations are underway in Serbia and Portugal, although the opening of new mines in both countries is considered problematic by the local population.

That securing imports of lithium is taken seriously by the European Union is evidenced by a renewed trade agreement with Chile that has been on the table since December 2022. This puts an end to most reciprocal export restrictions. The renewed agreement, which still—at least in June 2023—needs to be approved by the European Council and the European Parliament, means that European companies will be able to buy lithium at the price that applies within Chile.

Despite the rapidly increasing demand, lithium will not be depleted anytime soon. Identified lithium resources already amount to about 100 million tons,[28] but estimates of the amount of lithium in the continental Earth's crust that will eventually be extractable range from 500 million tons (low estimate) to 2,000 million tons (high estimate).[29] The distribution of indentified lithium resources around the world is quite different from the current distribution of lithium production (see Figure 5.7), and it is notable that the EU has as much lithium resources as China—both about 7% of world resources. The "lithium triangle" on the border between Chile, Bolivia, and Argentina contains about half of the world's lithium resources, while the United States and Canada also have a considerable 15% of the world's resources.

Assuming an eventual lithium recycling rate of 70%, there will still be sufficient lithium available in the continental Earth's crust for several hundred years, at the low estimate of lithium supply. If battery manufacturers are successful in increasing lithium recycling from batteries to 90%, then the available lithium reserves in the Earth's crust will be sufficient to supply the world for much longer. There is also a large supply of lithium dissolved in the oceans, which can be extracted economically at a cost about four to five times higher than

Five critical metals in electric cars 75

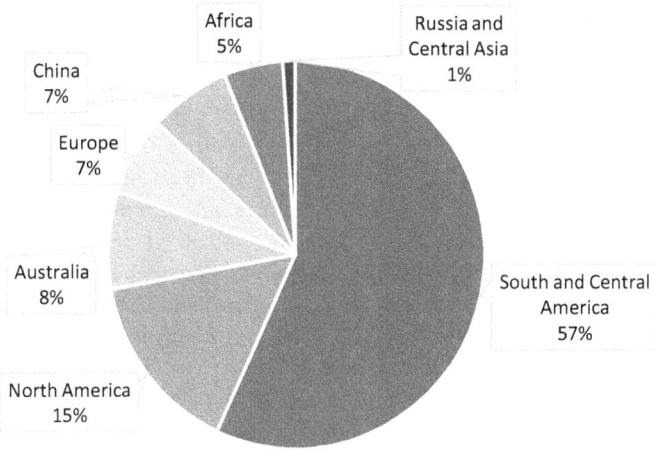

Figure 5.7 Distribution of identified lithium resources around the world. A total of about 100 million tons of lithium is involved.

Note: In Europe, reserves are found (in order of size) in Germany, the Czech Republic, Serbia, Spain, Portugal, Finland, and Austria.

Source: Data from the U.S. Geological Survey, Mineral Commodity Summaries, Lithium, 2023.

the extraction of lithium from the continental Earth's crust.[30] We therefore do not need to worry about lithium depletion for the time being.

> *China's Ganfeng Lithium is the largest producer of lithium salts in China and the second largest processor of lithium salts and lithium ore in the world after Chile's Sociedad Química y Minera (SQM). Ganfeng Lithium is the main supplier of lithium products to China's large lithium-ion battery manufacturers (BYD and CATL). Ganfeng is characteristic of Chinese entrepreneurship in the early twenty-first century. It was founded in 2000 by a former employee, Li Liangbin, of a Chinese state-owned company that supplied China's nuclear weapons industry with lithium mined in China. Li saw that demand for lithium in batteries was going to increase rapidly. Ganfeng concentrated on converting lithium salts and ores into lithium compounds suitable for application in batteries, which turned out to be an inspired move. As China's*

lithium resources were insufficient to meet demand, Li began to look for lithium suppliers outside China. Initially, he found these in the Chilean SQM and the American FMC. Starting in 2015, Ganfeng began participating in the exploitation of Australian lithium mines, enabling the further growth of Ganfeng to its current position as a global player in the lithium supply chain. Australia had a lot of experience in mining but not in the processing of lithium ore, and so the Chinese interest in their ore was welcomed by the Australian lithium mining companies. It was a win-win situation but with a major drawback—the ecological footprint of shipping the lithium ore thousands of miles and its processing in China using polluting coal. At the same time, the political relationship between Australia and China deteriorated. Ganfeng no longer wanted to depend solely on Australia for its lithium supply and so invested hundreds of millions of dollars in lithium production from brine in Argentina.

Much the same story can be told of the Chinese company Tianqi, which was able, in 2013, to acquire a share majority in Australia's largest lithium mine and then, in 2018, 24% of Chile's SQM, the world's largest lithium producer.

(Information from the book Volt Rush: The Winners and Losers in the Race to Go Green *byHenry Sanderson, 2022, Oneworld Publications, London.)*

Cobalt from Congo: a story of winners and losers

In days gone by, there was the gold rush. Looking for quick profit, adventurers descended on areas where it was said a vein of gold had been found. Sometimes a rumor was enough to stir hordes of seekers. Cobalt, one of the main components of the EV traction battery and batteries in cell phones, is the new gold of the Democratic Republic of Congo (DR Congo). In the south of the unstable country, in Katanga, there are nearly four million tons of the metal, almost half of the world's known cobalt reserves. The precious metal lies so close to the surface that tunnels are dug all over the ground, following the veins of ore. People also creep into the mines of the big companies at night to secretly dig up some cobalt ore for themselves.[31]

Cobalt is obtained for 38% as a by-product of nickel mining and for 60% as a by-product of copper mining. Only 2% of the world's produced cobalt is mined as the main product,[32] and only in DR Congo, Morocco, and the United States. More than 70% of the world's cobalt is produced in DR Congo. The main mining companies operating in DR Congo are Glencore (Switzerland), the Jinchuan Group (China), China Molybdenum Company Ltd (China), and Chemaf (from DR Congo itself). Artisanal[iii] cobalt mining, with or without copper, represents 10–30% of cobalt production in DR Congo,[33] so is not insignificant.

> *Glencore, based in Switzerland, is—in addition to being one of the world's largest producers of coal that is mainly mined in South Africa and Australia—also a major producer of copper, cobalt, and nickel. One part of Glencore is therefore engaged in activities that lead to increased CO_2 emissions, while the other part of the company produces the raw materials needed to stop the use of coal. This combination seems a stable revenue model for Glencore's shareholders. There are various stories about the relationship between Glencore and the Congolese rulers, but they have one thing in common: the enormous corruption surrounding the mining of cobalt in DR Congo. This corruption involves amounts of billions of dollars.*[34]

By far the most important application of cobalt is in batteries. Cobalt is also used in superalloys and other alloys for high-performance applications that must meet very high requirements in terms of hardness and resistance to extreme conditions of temperature and chemicals. There are numerous other smaller applications of cobalt (and its compounds), such as in catalysts in the chemical industry, in paints, in the ceramic industry, and even as a component of vitamin B12. Figure 5.8 shows the distribution of applications of cobalt in 2022.

Cobalt compounds were used as early as around 2000 BC in the Persian Empire to make blue pigments. At that time, of course, people

---

iii Artisanal cobalt mining is cobalt extraction without many professional tools on a small scale by individuals or a few people. It may involve children.

78 Five critical metals in electric cars

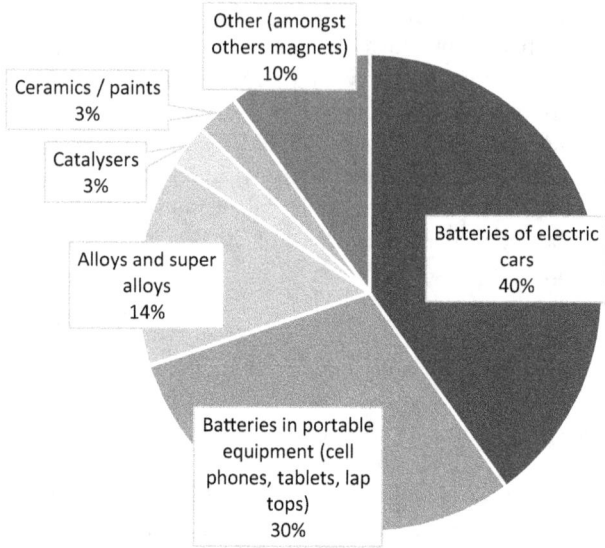

Figure 5.8 Applications of cobalt in 2022.

Source: Cobalt Institute, www.cobaltinstitute.org/wp-content/uploads/2023/05/Cobalt-Market-Report-2022_final-1.pdf, accessed May 11, 2023.

did not know they were using cobalt compounds. The element itself was not discovered until around 1730 by the Swede Georg Brandt. Cobalt is a silvery metal with a density of 8.9 kilograms per liter. It is therefore almost nine times heavier than water and almost as heavy as lead. Cobalt melts at a temperature of 1768°C.

> *The miserable conditions in the mines, the ongoing plundering of DR Congo since the country was privately owned by the Belgian King Leopold II, the huge levels of corruption, and the inability of successive Congolese governments to allow its people to benefit from the country's enormous mineral resources are described in detail in the book* Cobalt Red: How the Blood of the Congo Powers Our Lives, *by the American Siddharth Kara, an expert on modern slavery, human trafficking, and child labor.*

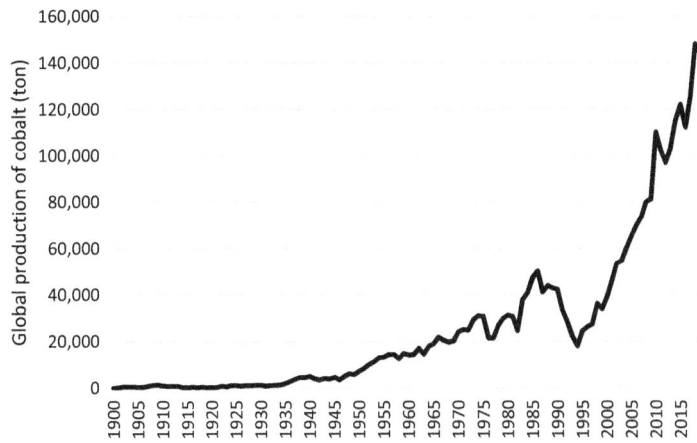

Figure 5.9 Global production of cobalt (tons per year).

Source: U.S. Geological Survey, 2019. Historical Statistics for Mineral and Material Commodities in the United States, Data Series 140, Cobalt.

In the short period between 2018 and 2022, the application of cobalt in EV batteries more than doubled, from less than 20% to 40% of all cobalt used. The other uses of cobalt also increased during that period, but not nearly as fast as in electric cars. The total production of cobalt is therefore increasing very rapidly, as shown in Figure 5.9.

The problems with working conditions in Congolese mines and the fact that 70% of the world's cobalt production is in DR Congo makes the supply of cobalt vulnerable. This has led cobalt users to look for suppliers in other countries and for substitute raw materials for cobalt in batteries. The Swiss company Glencore, which claims to extract cobalt only in a socially and environmentally responsible manner in professionally managed mines, has as a result become the preferred cobalt supplier of EV battery manufacturers, despite the corruption allegations.

The use of cobalt in lithium-ion batteries dates back only to the 1990s, when Sony began using lithium-ion batteries commercially in electronic gadgets such as the Walkman. The next acceleration came with the introduction of smartphones and tablets in around 2007-08. Each smartphone contains several grams of cobalt and each tablet several dozen grams. Next came electric bikes and scooters, but the

80 *Five critical metals in electric cars*

demand for cobalt really exploded with the introduction of the electric car. The battery pack of an electric car can contain up to 40 kilograms of cobalt, depending on the type of battery. Although cobalt-poor and cobalt-free batteries for electric cars are on the rise, such as LFP batteries, batteries containing cobalt will continue to be used for the time being.

Nevertheless, the cobalt industry has concerns about the possible overproduction of cobalt in the future, which will have a price-lowering effect. This is because most cobalt is extracted as a by-product of copper and nickel production, which means that the amount of cobalt produced is independent of the demand for cobalt. The supply of cobalt does not therefore necessarily match demand. A major additional uncertainty for cobalt producers is the future composition of traction batteries, which can also be made without cobalt.

In 2022, most of the world's cobalt by far was produced in DR Congo (70.1%). This was followed by Indonesia (5.4%), Russia (4.8%), and Australia (3.2%). Eight other countries were each responsible for 1–2% of the world's cobalt production: Canada, China, Cuba, Madagascar, Morocco, Papua New Guinea, the Philippines, and Turkey. DR Congo's annual cobalt production grew by a factor of 65 in 30 years, while world annual production grew "only" by a factor of seven over the same period. Despite rapidly growing demand, the real price paid for cobalt does not show a long-term upward trend, although there are short-term price fluctuations (see Figure 5.10). Cobalt reserves[iv] total 8,300 kilotons. These are reserves in the Earth's

---

iv The U.S. Geological Survey uses the following definitions:

1 Resources: A concentration of naturally occurring solid, liquid, or gaseous material in or on the Earth's crust in such form and amount that economic extraction of a commodity from the concentration is currently or potentially feasible.
2 Undiscovered resources: Resources whose existence and amount are estimated based on geological conditions and data with respect to similar deposits of the same or other materials.
3 Identified resources: Resources whose location, grade, quality, and quantity are known or estimated from specific geologic evidence. Identified resources include economic, marginally economic, and subeconomic components.
4 Reserve base: That part of an identified resource that meets specified minimum physical and chemical criteria related to current mining and production practices, including those for grade, quality, thickness, and depth.
5 Reserves: That part of the reserve base which could be economically extracted or produced at the time of determination.

Five critical metals in electric cars 81

Figure 5.10 Inflation-adjusted price of cobalt expressed in $22 per ton.

Note: Prices of 2019 are based on the price of cobalt in the United States. The price between 2020 and 2022 is the price on the London Metal Exchange, also expressed in $22. Inflation rates are taken from the U.S. Bureau of Labor Statistics. The Consumer Price Index was used to account for inflation.

Source: U.S. Geological Survey, 2019. Historical Statistics for Mineral and Material Commodities in the United States, Data Series 140, Cobalt.

crust that can currently be mined commercially. Almost half of these reserves are in DR Congo (see Figure 5.11).

The identified cobalt resources in the continental Earth's crust are 25,000 kilotons, so about a factor of three more. I estimate the undiscovered amount of cobalt in the continental Earth's crust that could potentially be mined in the future to be another factor of eight to over factor of 100 higher, so between 200,000 and three million kilotons,[35] and therefore a multiple of the currently recorded reserves. Furthermore, there is still a significant amount of cobalt present at the bottom of the ocean in manganese nodules and manganese crusts. Cobalt can therefore not yet be considered a geologically scarce material.

It would make sense for DR Congo, like Indonesia with respect to nickel, to refine cobalt that it mines itself. But, as a senior manager of Gécamines, DR Congo's national mining company, explained: "In Congo, we don't have enough electricity to refine cobalt."[36] Currently, about three-quarters of the world's cobalt ore is refined to battery grade in China.

82 Five critical metals in electric cars

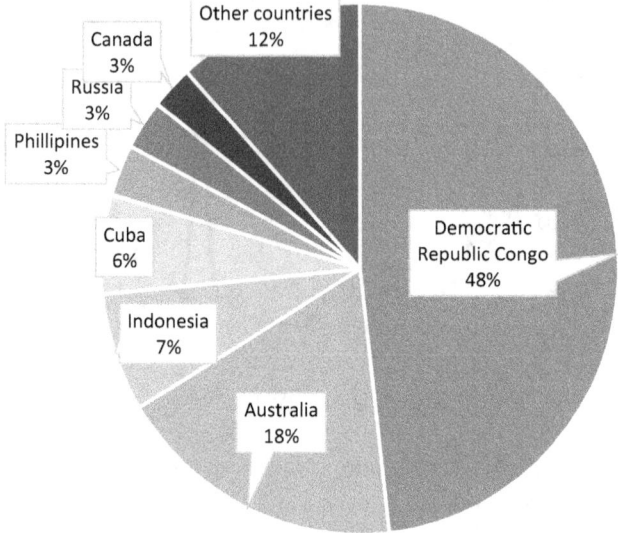

Figure 5.11 Distribution of cobalt reserves in the world in 2022.

Source: U.S. Geological Survey, January 2023. Mineral Commodity Summaries, Cobalt.

The recycling rate of cobalt depends on the type of application. Recovery from cobalt alloys and superalloys can be as high as 80%, but virtually no cobalt is recovered from ceramics and catalysts. In terms of cobalt from batteries, consumer electronics such as cell phones, tablets, and laptops are currently of particular interest. The EU Batteries Regulation has set mandatory collection rates as high as 73% by 2030, with a minimum cobalt recovery rate of 95% as of December 31, 2031.

> *While Glencore mainly operates the large copper and cobalt mines in DR Congo, Chinese companies such as Huayou Cobalt tend to buy cobalt from local traders, who in turn purchase the ore from individual miners or small companies who mine artisanally, especially in the region around Kolwezi, without proper safety measures and using child labor. From the children's*

hands, the cobalt ore eventually reaches Quzhou in China, where it is processed into battery-grade cobalt compounds. In 2019, the Huayou Cobalt plant in Quzhou had a capacity of 30,000 tons per year—a third of the world demand at the time.[37] The Quzhou plant also recovers cobalt from the cathodes of discarded battery packs from electric buses. Huayou Cobalt was established in 2002 with the goal of supplying cobalt to the ceramic industry, which today plays only a minor role in terms of cobalt applications. With insufficient cobalt being mined in China itself, Huayou Cobalt's founder soon explored cobalt supply options in DR Congo. This was the time of huge growth in the sale of cell phones, all of which contained rechargeable lithium-ion batteries, which required cobalt. The bulk of the production of these phones took place in China, so cobalt, lithium, and nickel were in high demand. Huayou Cobalt was therefore not the only Chinese company trying to buy cobalt in DR Congo; by the end of 2013, it was one of about 100 Chinese companies doing so.[38] Huayou Cobalt was able to take a leading position, buying up cobalt from Chinese middlemen. Ultimately, this is how most of the artisanally mined cobalt in DR Congo ends up in China via Huayou Cobalt.

The bulk of cobalt mined industrially, for example by Glencore, is also refined in China. In 2019, 90% of all cobalt from DR Congo was processed in China.[39] However, not only cobalt from DR Congo is transported to China for refining; in 2021, China was refining 75% of all the cobalt in the world.[40] Initially, Huayou Cobalt was an important cobalt supplier for electronic devices with rechargeable batteries built by Sony, Nokia, Samsung, and Apple. Later, it became an important supplier to electric car manufacturers such as BYD and Volkswagen, as well as to producers of EV battery packs, such as LG Chem, Samsung SDI, and CATL.[41]

In 2016, Amnesty International published a report on the deplorable working conditions in the mining of the cobalt purchased by Huayou Cobalt in DR Congo. Although the Amnesty International report forced Huayou Cobalt to critically review its operations in the country, it is unclear whether much has changed in practice in the cobalt mines. The buyers source

> cobalt from middlemen, who mix small batches of different origins to meet desired specifications. It is therefore often unclear exactly where the cobalt in a given batch comes from, whether children have worked to produce it, what the working conditions are, and whether miners are paid a decent wage.

This will result in a cobalt recycling rate from portable batteries in Europe of nearly 70% as of 2032. EV traction batteries will be added to this in the future, from which almost all the cobalt will be recoverable. Since cobalt will be used mainly in batteries, certainly in the near future, it is to be expected that much of the cobalt used will be recycled, at least in Europe.

War on the nickel exchange

The London Metal Exchange is one of the oldest in the world. Traders, mostly men (who are required to wear a tie or risk a £500 fine), sit in a circle and buy and sell metals, shouting and gesticulating wildly. The exchange will soon have existed for 150 years, but what happened in the spring of 2022 had rarely been seen.

Russia is an exporter of nickel. In March 2022, when the European Union responded to the war in Ukraine with sanctions against Russia, many traders feared a nickel shortage. As a consequence, the price of the metal—which is essential for stainless steel and batteries—skyrocketed. On March 8, stock exchange management had no choice but to halt trading, as the price rose by 250% in one day, even briefly touching $100,000 for a ton of nickel.[42] Previous trades that day were reversed.

Meanwhile, writing in March 2023, exactly one year later, the price is $24,000 per ton of nickel—still quite high, but well within the range over the last century. Calm has returned to the nickel exchange, which is only logical, as although Russia was the main nickel producer until 2013, it has since been surpassed by the Philippines and Indonesia. Indonesia now produces almost eight times more nickel than Russia, and the Philippines 1.5 times more. Indonesia's reserves are three times higher than Russia's, and Brazil and Australia also have significantly higher nickel reserves than Russia.

Nickel ore and its processing products are transported by trucks, trains, and ocean-going vessels, not by pipelines, which can be shut down or sabotaged. So, while the stock market panic was not based on actual shortages in the market, it can be seen as an indicator of nickel's importance to the economy and the energy transition. Indonesia understands this well, and Hyundai opened a plant in Jakarta in 2022 for the production of its new electric car model the Ionic 5. In the same year, Chinese battery manufacturer CATL signed an agreement for a new battery plant in Indonesia, Mitsubishi promised to expand in Indonesia, and Toyota will also open a plant there. Tesla has also signed major nickel contracts in Indonesia. Furthermore, Indonesia reports that negotiations with the Chinese electric car manufacturer BYD are in the final stages.[43]

> *The search for nickel is being taken to extremes. The Luxembourg company Aperam has set up a division focusing on the production of bionickel, that is, nickel from plants. The plant yellow tuft* (Alyssum murale) *is nickel-loving and can extract up to 300 kilograms of nickel per hectare per year from the soil for up to 30 years.*[44] *This way of producing nickel will probably not make much of a contribution to solving any nickel shortages, rather to the depletion of agricultural land, but of course it looks good for the big stainless steel producer Aperam, which is part of Mittal.*

Nickel is quite a heavy metal, and one liter of pure nickel weighs 8.9 kilograms—about the same as copper. Unlike copper, nickel is used almost exclusively in alloys. The main application for nickel is in the production of various types of stainless steel and in all kinds of nickel alloys with other non-ferrous metals; these currently total 85% of nickel applications (like iron, nickel is a magnetic metal). The properties of nickel make alloys stronger and more resistant to high temperatures and corrosive conditions. For example, nickel is widely used in alloys in steam turbines for power generation and in aircraft, and computer hard drives are coated with nickel. The use of nickel in lithium-ion battery cathodes is growing rapidly and may surpass the other applications in the future. Currently, about 5% of nickel goes to automotive batteries, and 95% to other applications, including an increasing amount in steel parts of wind turbines. If the International Energy Agency's NZE Scenario comes true, the share of nickel in battery cathodes could grow to 45% of total nickel consumption by 2050. Other uses of nickel will also increase. As a result, nickel production will have to increase by 6.5% per year for the time being, as shown in Chapter 3. Nickel is also used to galvanize metal surfaces (nickel plating) and numerous other applications, such as in chemicals, catalysts, ceramic materials, and coins.

> *The gold-colored center of a two-euro coin consists of 75% copper and 25% nickel, while the silver edge consists of 75% copper, 20% zinc, and 5% nickel. In a one-euro coin, this is exactly the other way around.*

Cathodes of lithium-ion batteries usually contain a mixture of lithium, cobalt, nickel, and manganese compounds. Because of the problems with cobalt from DR Congo (child labor, unsafe working conditions, war lords, environmental pollution), producers of lithium-ion batteries would like to have as little cobalt in the cathode as possible. This can be done by making the mixture richer in nickel, which will likely lead in the short term to the use of nickel in lithium-ion batteries increasing even faster than the use of lithium-ion batteries themselves. Although things may be looking up for nickel producers and processors right now, this is, however, unlikely to continue as nickel will no longer be needed in EV batteries at all if the LFP battery and then the ASSB battery become a success. However, nickel consumption in other applications, in particular in a variety of steel and non-ferrous alloys, will continue to rise with increasing world prosperity. This will probably mean an annual increase in production in line with that between 1980 and 2020, so about 3% per year, which is a lot less than the 6.5% per year that would be needed if future car batteries were to continue to have roughly the same composition as those in 2023. This may even need to be temporarily higher due to the replacement of cobalt with nickel.

> *China itself produces only 3% of the world's nickel, and its nickel reserves are even less than 2% of world reserves, while nearly 20% of the Earth's inhabitants are Chinese nationals. It is therefore very important for China to secure imports of nickel, or nickel-containing semi-finished products. In that context, China is very active in Indonesia, the world's leading nickel producer with the largest reserves. Chinese companies have long been active in Sulawesi and Halmahera, where Indonesian nickel mining is concentrated, and have built refineries and smelters, and even established a metallurgy school and a nickel museum. President Widodo of Indonesia banned all exports of metal ore in 2020, so that only processed raw materials may be exported. Since then, the value of Indonesia's nickel exports has increased dramatically. Chinese battery manufacturers GEM and CATL set up a joint production line in Sulawesi in 2022, producing the high-purity nickel needed to manufacture car batteries. The presence of Chinese companies is not entirely without tensions in Indonesia, however, as a good portion of the work is done by Chinese workers.*[45]

In November 2022, Indonesia—as the main nickel-producing country in the world—suggested creating a nickel cartel to strengthen the interests of nickel-producing countries and achieve price control, similar to the Organization of Petroleum Exporting Countries (OPEC). It remains to be seen whether that will happen, but it marks the importance of nickel for the global economy and for Indonesia.

Figure 5.12 shows how nickel production has shifted in recent decades from Russia to Indonesia and the Philippines. In 1994, Russia was the dominant nickel producer with about 25% of world nickel production, but that has now fallen to 7% of world production, while Indonesia's share has increased over the same period, from 9% in 1994 to 48% of world nickel production in 2022. Total nickel production has tripled over the same period (see Figure 5.13).

Nickel production in Indonesia is largely carried out by PT Vale Indonesia, which is part of the Brazilian multinational Vale and the Indonesian state-owned Aneka Tambang. Nickel production grew by 3.1% per year between 1980 and 2020, representing a doubling in production every 23 years. The growth rate has increased even more in recent years: 8.5% annually between 2017 and 2022. Despite

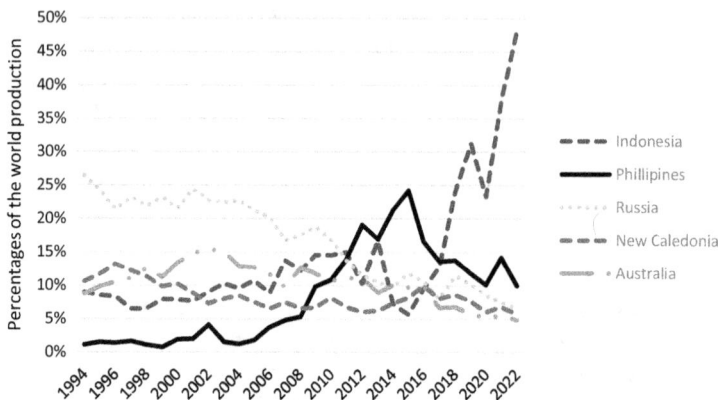

Figure 5.12 Share of major nickel-producing countries in world production between 1994 and 2022. World nickel production increased from 1.1 million tons in 1994 to 3.3 million tons in 2022. Data from the U.S. Geological Survey.

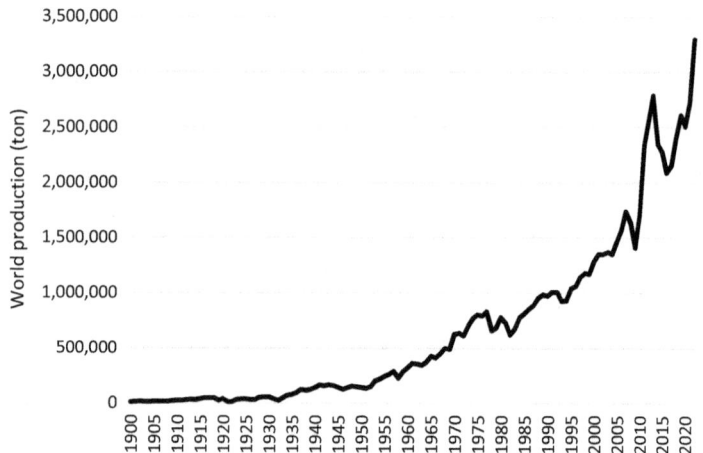

Figure 5.13 World nickel production in tons. Data from the U.S. Geological Survey.

Figure 5.14 Evolution of the real nickel price between 1900 and 2022, expressed in US dollars of 2022. Data from the U.S. Geological Survey.

fluctuations, the real nickel price shows no clear upward trend (see Figure 5.14).

The real nickel price has varied between about $10 and $30 per kilogram over the last century (based on the dollar value in 2022), barring some price spikes. The high nickel prices in the periods 1986–1988 and 2006–2010 can both be explained by a combination of high demand and lagging supply. This was due, fortunately, not to wars, but to a temporary mismatch between supply and demand. In March 2022, the nickel price briefly shot through the roof of the chart to a high of $100,000, as we saw at the beginning of this section, but this was short-lived. Despite its greater availability in the Earth's crust, nickel is more expensive than copper, mainly because its production requires about three times as much energy as production of the same amount of copper.

The world's largest nickel companies are listed in Table 5.3. In part, they are the same companies as for copper (Glencore, BHP, and AngloAmerican).

Table 5.3 Largest nickel companies in 2021

Company	Country	Percentage of world nickel production	Nickel mining and nickel refining	Nickel refining
Norilsk Nickel	Russia	18%	Russia, South Africa	Finland
Vale SA	Brazil	14%	Brazil, Canada, Indonesia	New Caledonia, United Kingdom
Tsingshan	China	8%	Indonesia	
Glencore	Switzerland		Canada, Australia, Norway, New Caledonia	
BHP	Australia		Australia, Colombia	
Anglo American	United Kingdom		Brazil	
Eramet	France		New Caledonia	Indonesia, France
South 32	Australia		Australia	
IGO Ltd	Australia		Australia	
Terra Fame	Finland		Finland	
Metallurgical Corporation of China (MCC)	China		Indonesia, Papua New Guinea	
Nickel Asia Corporation	Philippines		Philippines	

> *The large amount of energy required for nickel production, especially from laterite, is a concern for electric car manufacturers. Indonesia will have to quickly switch from coal-fired power plants, which are currently used to supply energy for nickel production, to clean energy from hydropower and solar panels to reduce the carbon footprint of nickel in batteries.*

The average nickel concentration in the Earth's crust is 68 parts per million, or 0.0068%. This means that nickel is slightly more prevalent in the Earth's crust than copper. The nickel concentration in nickel ore is also somewhat higher than the copper concentration in copper ore. Nevertheless, the annual extraction of nickel is currently seven times lower than that of copper.

Like copper, nickel is largely mined in opencast mines. Large craters are formed in the landscape, with huge trucks bringing the nickel ore up the sides on narrow steep roads. The nickel-containing mineral is then separated as much as possible from the rock in which the nickel ore is contained. There are two main types of nickel ore: the first is a mineral based on oxides of nickel and iron, called laterite, which occurs mainly in regions closer to the equator (the Philippines, Indonesia, New Caledonia, Australia, Brazil). The second type of nickel is a mineral based on nickel sulfide that occurs mainly in more arctic regions such as Russia and Canada. The nickel concentration in sulfide deposits is between 0.2% and 2%,[46] and in laterite ore between 1.0% and 1.6%.[47] Manganese nodules on the ocean floor also contain quite a bit of nickel, an estimated 1.7%.

For its application in batteries, it is necessary to use Class 1 nickel with more than 99.8% nickel. Class 1 nickel can be made more easily from sulfide ore than from oxide ore. Since about 20% of this is supplied by Russia,[48] this may have been part of the reason for the tremendous increase in nickel prices in 2022. Nevertheless, battery-grade nickel is also increasingly being made from nickel oxide ore, for example in Indonesia, where China's CATL is setting up a battery plant based on Class 1 nickel made from nickel oxide ore using the high-pressure acid leaching (HPAL) process.

Nickel ranks ninth in terms of occurrence in the Earth's crust, along with chromium and zinc and after aluminum (1,250 times more), iron (750 times more), magnesium (250 times more), titanium (75 times more), manganese (12.5 times more), barium (six times more), strontium (five times more), and rare earths (two times more).

> *Nickel was discovered relatively late, in 1751 by the Swedish baron Axel Fredrik Cronstedt. Nickel was used in coins from the mid-nineteenth century. The U.S. nickel, which has been in circulation since 1866, is a five-cent coin and consists of 25% nickel and 75% copper. It contains 1.1 grams of nickel and 3.75 grams of copper. Depending on the price of copper and nickel, the metal value of the coin sometimes rises above $0.05 per coin, making it attractive to melt down for sale to non-ferrous traders. This practice was formally banned by the U.S. Mint in 2007.*

The distribution of nickel reserves, which total more than 100 million tons, is shown in Figure 5.15. The total identified amount of recoverable nickel in the Earth's crust is estimated by U.S. Geological Survey to be 300 million tons.

The most optimistic estimate of the ultimate extractable amount of nickel in the Earth's crust is 8,000 million tons, and the most

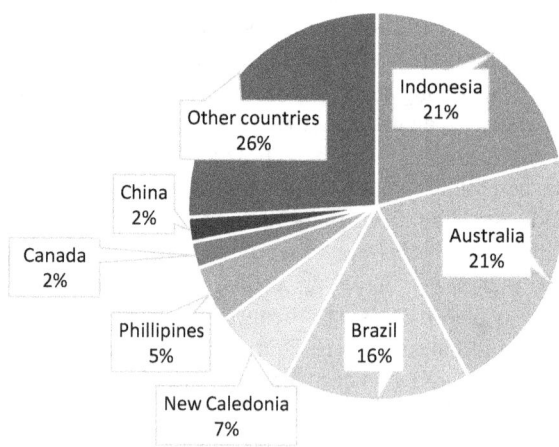

Figure 5.15 Distribution of nickel reserves in 2023 (total reserves were over 100 million tons in 2023). Data from the U.S. Geological Survey.

pessimistic estimate 1,000 million tons.[49] In 2022, nickel extraction from the Earth's crust was 3.3 million tons. It therefore looks as though we can continue as we are for some time: no problems yet in "the foreseeable future" according to the U.S. Geological Survey. But with an increase in nickel consumption of at least 6.5% per year, which is required to keep up with the necessary pace of the energy transition, extraction will rise frighteningly fast. At such a rate, nickel extraction will increase to over 19 million tons by 2050, nearly six times what it was in 2020. If the pessimistic scenario of 1,000 million tons is true, there would still be enough for 50 years after 2050, at least if the annual 6.5% increase in production stopped in 2050. But why should it stop and not continue to double every 23 years? After all, the fair scenario in which all countries have become as prosperous as the European Union is far from being achieved in 2050.

Could recycling be the solution? Currently, 57% of the nickel in end-of-life products is recycled, which is already quite a high percentage. This is because nickel is mostly found in high-grade steel and other expensive alloys. When separating metals at the recycling stage, it pays to properly sort nickel alloys by type and concentration and then mix the fractions in such a way that they can be used directly in the new production of nickel alloys. Nevertheless, 14% of nickel is still downcycled to lower-value or non-functional applications, mainly because it is not yet sufficiently cost-effective to isolate nickel from waste products with a low nickel concentration or to use it directly in the nickel cycle. Nickel substitution is difficult in most applications, with only the replacement of nickel in automotive batteries looking promising.

Greenland and its rare earths are not for sale

President Donald Trump had a brilliant idea in 2019, or so he thought. He wanted to buy Greenland from Denmark. Trump considered it "a great real estate transaction." In Denmark, they laughed heartily about it. "I hope this is not meant seriously," said Danish Prime Minister Mette Frederiksen. For Trump, that was the reason to cancel a visit to the generally very America-friendly country. "Based on Prime Minister Mette Frederiksen's comments, that she would have no interest in discussing the purchase of Greenland, I will be postponing our meeting scheduled in two weeks for another time," Trump wrote on X, formerly known as Twitter.

The question is why Trump wanted Greenland so badly. One reason could be that Greenland has relatively abundant resources, including an ample supply of rare earths that are used for example in wind turbine and electric motor magnets. China is currently the main supplier of rare earths, and the Kvanefjeld mine in southwest Greenland may prove to be the most important source of these elements outside China.

How rare are they really, these rare earth metals? As it turns out, much less than their name suggests. Of the metals, they rank eighth in quantity in the Earth's crust, after aluminum, iron, magnesium, titanium, manganese, barium, and strontium, and are therefore less rare than better-known metals such as copper, zinc, and nickel. They are called "rare" because there are not many highly concentrated occurrences from which they can be easily extracted.

The rare earths are scandium, yttrium, and the 15 lanthanides. In the periodic table of elements, they are in column three from the left. The lanthanides are lanthanum, cerium, praseodymium, neodymium, promethium, samarium, europium, gadolinium, terbium, dysprosium, holmium, erbium, thulium, ytterbium, and lutetium. The most abundant rare earth, cerium, with an average concentration of 68 ppm, is more abundant in the Earth's crust than copper and lead and as abundant as nickel. The least common rare earth (lutetium) is still significantly more common than gold. However, these are averages. The difference with lead and gold is that rare earths occur little in concentrated form, so the number of economically interesting deposits is comparatively small.

About 300,000 tons of rare earths were produced in 2022, expressed as rare earth oxide equivalent, with about 85% rare earth content. China was by far the largest producer, with about 210,000 tons, or 70% of the world total. See Figure 5.16. Because rare earths are chemically similar, they always occur in combination, although the mix varies from one mine to another. There are therefore no separate mines for neodymium, for example.

The composition of the rare earth metals mix at the Mountain Pass mine in the United States on the California–Nevada border, which in 1990 still accounted for 40% of world rare earth production, is as follows: 48% cerium, 35% lanthanum, 11% neodymium, 4% praseodymium, 1% samarium, 0.2% gadolinium, 0.1% europium, 0.03% dysprosium, and 0.6% other rare earths.[50]

Five critical metals in electric cars 95

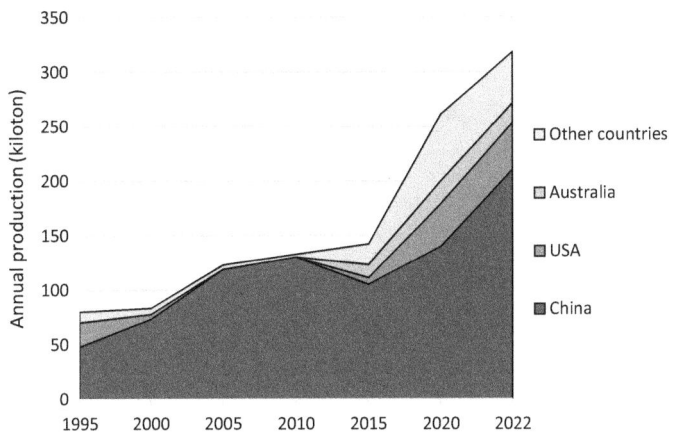

Figure 5.16 Annual rare earth production. Production is expressed in rare earth oxide equivalent. The rare earth content is about 85%.

Source: Data from the U.S. Geological Survey. Mineral Commodity Summaries, Rare Earths, 1996–2023.

Global reserves of rare earths were estimated at 130 million tons rare earth oxide equivalent in 2023, of which 44 million tons were in China. Vietnam is second with 22 million tons, and Brazil and Russia take shared third place with estimated reserves of 21 million tons each.[51] Of the other countries, India, Australia, the United States, Greenland, Tanzania, Canada, and South Africa have the largest reserves (in descending order), with a combined 17.4 million tons. Returning to Donald Trump's peculiar proposal to buy Greenland, estimated reserves in Greenland are 1.5 million tons rare earth oxide equivalent, with a current value of about $20 billion. The ultimate extractable quantity is, however, likely to be considerably larger. It is notable that China currently accounts for 70% of global rare earth production, while China's share of world rare earth reserves is only about one-third. See Figure 5.17. Based on parallels with other metals, I estimate the ultimate extractable amount of rare earths in the Earth's crust to be somewhere between 3,500 million tons and 25,000 million tons rare earth oxide equivalent.[52]

In January 2023, the Swedish mining company LKAB announced that it had found a large deposit of rare earths near Kiruna in Sweden.

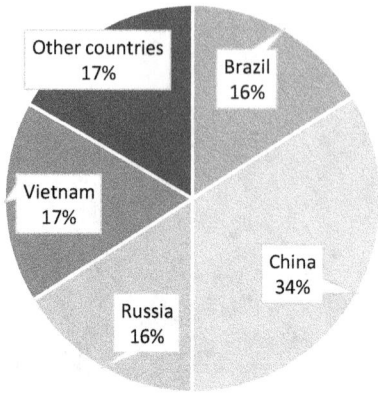

Figure 5.17 Estimated distribution of rare earth reserves.

According to preliminary investigations, there are about one million tons of rare earth oxides in the ground, making it the largest find in Europe. In recent years, rare earth production in China has been gradually concentrated in a few companies. Of these, China Rare Earth Group is the largest. This state-owned company handles 70% of rare earth production in China.[53]

Despite significant fluctuations, the real price of rare earths has not really increased over time (see Figure 7.2 in Chapter 7). The price of the unrefined but concentrated mixture of rare earths, as it comes out of the mine, has remained between $15 and $25 per kilogram in recent years, expressed in the dollar value of 2022.[54] Table 5.4 gives an impression of the price of the separate rare earths.

The price of different rare earths varies quite a bit. There are two reasons for this. First, some rare earths are much more common than others. Second, market demand varies. For example, the demand for neodymium and dysprosium for magnets is particularly high. That means that cerium, for example, with fewer applications and a higher occurrence in the Earth's crust, is priced much lower than neodymium. To give an example, the rare earth ore at Mountain Pass in the United States contains four times less neodymium than cerium and as much as 1,600 times less dysprosium than cerium.

In this book, rare earths receive attention because they are used in permanent magnets in wind turbines and EV motors. This mainly

Five critical metals in electric cars 97

Table 5.4 Prices of rare earth oxides in US dollars per kilogram (purity >99.5%)

	2005	2010	2011	2012	2013	2014	2015	2016	2017	2018	2019	2020	2021
Yttrium	88	50	165	88	25	16	8	4	3	3	3	3	5
Lanthanum	23	38	100	23	8	5	3	2	2	2	2	2	2
Cerium	19	30	100	23	8	5	3	2	2	2	2	2	2
Praseodymium	37	60	225	115	94	121	76	52	65	63			
Neodymium	29	63	270	117	70	63	48	40	50	50	45	49	49
Samarium	360	175	118	62	14	7	3	2	2	2			
Europium	990	1,400	3,300	2,440	1,130	822	344	74	77	53	35	31	31
Gadolinium	130	165	239	92	47	47	21	20	37	44			
Terbium	535	1,400	2,750	1,950	949	713	564	415	501	455	507	670	1,300
Dysprosium	120	310	1,600	1,010	540	395	279	198	189	179	239	261	400

Source: U.S. Geological Survey. Various editions of the Mineral Yearbook.
Note: Prices are not adjusted for inflation.

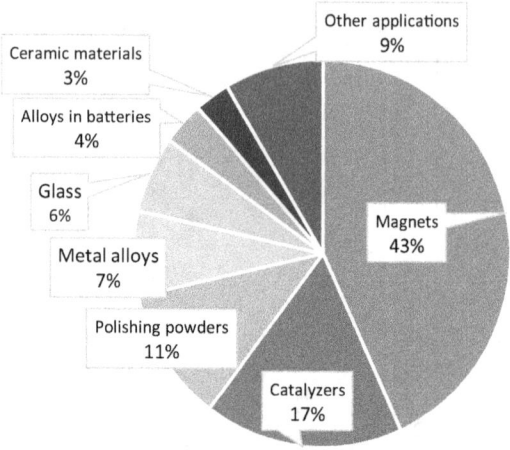

Figure 5.18 Applications of rare earths in 2021.

Source: Government of Canada, Rare earths elements facts, https://natural-resources.canada.ca/our-natural-resources/minerals-mining/minerals-metals-facts/rare-earth-elements-facts/20522.

concerns neodymium and dysprosium, but other rare earth metals are also used. A 5 MW wind turbine with a permanent magnet may contain as much as 900 kilograms of neodymium and an average electric car contains one kilogram of rare earths. Every electronic device also contains a few grams of rare earth metal, mostly because of its magnetic properties. Dysprosium, neodymium, praseodymium, and terbium are mainly used in wind turbines, while neodymium and dysprosium are mainly used in EV motors. Incidentally, permanent magnets are used in only a quarter of wind turbines.[55] Nevertheless, the global use of rare earths is rising rapidly because of their application in magnets. By 2021, almost half of the rare earths produced were for magnetic applications, compared to just 20% five years earlier in 2016. See Figure 5.18.

Recycling of rare earths is still in its infancy, in part because of the type of applications, from most of which it is costly to recover rare earths separately. Nevertheless, rare earth recovery is expected to increase in the future, particularly from larger objects such as wind turbines and electric cars. The European Commission proposes that by 2030 at least 15% of the rare earths in permanent magnets should be recycled material. That means a significant recycling infrastructure for rare earths must be established by then.

> *The draft Critical Raw Materials Act proposed by the European Commission sets the goal of self-extracting a minimum of 10% of strategic raw materials for the EU by 2030, self-refining a minimum of 40% of strategic raw materials, having a minimum of 15% of the use of strategic raw materials in the European Union be recycled, and limiting the import of a strategic raw material from one particular country to a maximum of 65%. The strategic raw materials are bismuth, boron for metallurgy, cobalt, copper, gallium, germanium, lithium for batteries, magnesium metal, manganese for batteries, natural graphite for batteries, nickel for batteries, platinum metals, rare earth metals for magnets, silicon metal, titanium metal, and tungsten.*

Notes

1 www.nrc.nl/nieuws/2007/01/18/barbaarse-koperdieven-roven-beeld-van-rodin-11261606-a150973
2 *Volkskrant*, June 19, 2023.
3 "How copper drives electric vehicles," www.copper.org/publications/pub_list/pdf/A6192_ElectricVehicles-Infographic.pdf, August 5, 2022.
4 "If electrons are the lifeblood of a modern economy, copper makes up its blood vessels": Kerr, R.A., 2014. The coming copper peak, *Science*, 343 (6172), 722–724.
5 Copper Alliance, 2019. Global 2018 Semis End Use Data Set, https://copperalliance.org/trends-and-innovations/data-set/, retrieved on January 14, 2019.
6 U.S. Geological Survey, 2009. Copper—A Metal for Ages, Fact Sheet 2009–3031.
7 U.S. Geological Survey, 2021. Copper Statistics, May 3 and Mineral Commodity Summary, January 2024.
8 The US Bureau of Labor Statistics' Consumer Price Index was used to account for inflation.
9 Henckens, M.L.C.M., van Ierland, E.C., Driessen, P.P.J., and Worrell, E., 2016. Geological scarcity, market price trends and future generations, *Resources Policy*, 49, 102–111.
10 Kerr, 2014. The coming copper peak, Science 343 (6172) 722–724; Northey, S., Mohr, S., Mudd, G., Weng, Z., and Giurco, D., 2014. Modeling

future copper ore grade decline based on a detailed assessment of copper resources and mining, *Resources, Conservation, Recycling*, 83, 190–201.
11. Northey, Mohr, Mudd, Weng and Giurco, 2014. Modeling future copper ore grade decline based on a detailed assessment of copper resources and mining, Resources, Conservation, Recycling, 83, 190–201
12. Skinner, B.J., 1987. Supplies of geochemically scarce metals. In: *Resources and World Development*, MacLaren, D.J. and Skinner, B.J., eds., John Wiley and Sons, Chichester UK, pp. 305–325; Gordon, R.B., Koopmans, J.J., Nordhaus, W.B., and Skinner, B.J., 2016. *Towards a New Iron Age.* Harvard University Press, Cambridge, MA.
13. Bardi, U., 2014. *Extracted. How the quest for mineral wealth is plundering the planet. The past, present, and future of global mineral depletion.* A report for the Club of Rome. Chelsea Green Publishing, Originally published in German as Der geplünderte Planet in 2013 by oekom verlag GmbH, Munich.
14. U.S. Geological Survey, 2018. Assessment of undiscovered copper resources of the world, 2015, Scientific Investigations Report 2018-5160, Version December 21, 2021.
15. U.S. Geological Survey, Mineral commodity summaries, Copper.
16. Kuipers, K.J.J., van Oers, L.F.C.M., Verboon, M., and van der Voet, E., 2018. Assessing environmental implications associated with global copper demand and supply scenarios from 2010 to 2050. *Global Environmental Change*, 49, 106–115.
17. Fridleifsson, I.B., Bertani, R., Huenges, E., Lund, J.W., Ragnarsson, A., and Rybach, L., 2008. The possible role and contribution of geothermal energy to the mitigation of climate change. In: *Proceedings of the IPPC Scoping Meeting on Renewable Energy Sources*, Luebeck, Germany, January 15–20, Hohmeyer, O. and Trittin, T., eds., pp. 59-80.
18. U.S. Geological Survey, 2018. Assessment of undiscovered copper.
19. Henckens, T., 2021. *Governance of the World's Mineral Resources. Beyond the Foreseeable Future*, Elsevier, Amsterdam.
20. Henckens, T., 2021. *Governance of the World's Mineral Resources. Beyond the Foreseeable Future*, Elsevier, Amsterdam.
21. Henckens, T., 2021. *Governance of the World's Mineral Resources. Beyond the Foreseeable Future*, Elsevier, Amsterdam.
22. Henckens, T., 2021. *Governance of the World's Mineral Resources. Beyond the Foreseeable Future*, Elsevier, Amsterdam.
23. Evans, R.K., 2012, An overabundance of lithium? 4th Lithium Supply & Markets Conference. Buenos Aires, Argentina, January 23–25 (Presentation).
24. U.S. Geological Survey, 2018. *Minerals Yearbook, Lithium.*
25. https://about.bnef.com/blog/china-dominates-the-lithium-ion-battery-sup ply-chain-but-europe-is-on-the-rise/, retrieved March 14, 2023.

26 Bae, H. and Kim, Y., 2021. Technologies of lithium recycling from waste lithium ion batteries: an overview, *Materials Advances*, 2, 3234–3250.
27 Gregoir, L., 2022. Metals for clean energy. Report by the Katholieke Universiteit Leuven for Eurometaux.
28 US Geological Survey, 2023, Mineral Commodity Summaries, Lithium.
29 Henckens, T., 2021. *Governance of the World's Mineral Resources. Beyond the Foreseeable Future*, Elsevier, Amsterdam.
30 Yaksic, A. and Tilton, J.E., 2009, Using the cumulative availability curve to assess the threat of mineral depletion, *Resources Policy*, 34, 185–194.
31 Niarchos, N., 2021. The dark side of Congo's Cobalt Rush, *The New Yorker*, May 31.
32 U.S. Geological Survey, Mineral Commodity Summaries, Cobalt, January 2023; "Growing demand for cobalt sourcing—driven by its crucial role in enabling electric mobility and the green economy—puts the spotlight the way this critical mineral is sourced," www.cobaltinstitute.org/responsible-sourcing/, April 5, 2023.
33 International Energy Agency, 2022. Global Supply Chains of EV Batteries; Kara, S., 2023. *Cobalt Red: How the Blood of The Congo Powers Our Lives*. St. Martin's Publishing Group, New York.
34 "DR Congo stands to lose $3.71 billion in mining deals with Dan Gertler," www.raid-uk.org/blog/drc-congo-stands-lose-3-71-billion-mining-deals-dan-gertler, May 12, 2021, accessed April 3, 2023.
35 Henckens, T., 2021. *Governance of the World's Mineral Resources. Beyond the Foreseeable Future*, Elsevier, Amsterdam.
36 Kara, 2023. *Cobalt Red*: How the Blood of The Congo Powers Our Lives. St. Martin's Publishing Group, New York.
37 Sanderson, H., 2021. *Volt Rush: The Winners and Losers in the Race to Go Green*, Oneworld Publications, London, p. 126.
38 Sanderson, H., 2021, *Volt Rush: The Winners and Losers in the Race to Go Green*, Oneworld Publications, London, p. 126.
39 Sanderson, H., 2021, *Volt Rush: The Winners and Losers in the Race to Go Green*, Oneworld Publications, London, p. 126.
40 Kara, S., 2023. *Cobalt Red: How the Blood of The Congo Powers Our Lives*. St. Martin's Publishing Group, New York.
41 Sanderson, H., 2021, *Volt Rush: The Winners and Losers in the Race to Go Green*, Oneworld Publications, London, p. 126.
42 Koenis, C., Unprecedented nickel boom flattens London trade, NRC, March 21, 2022. www.nrc.nl/nieuws/2022/03/21/ongekende-nikkelhausse-legt-handel-in-londen-plat-a4103050
43 *De Volkskrant*, February 7, 2023.
44 *Dagblad van het Noorden*, February 18, 2023.
45 Financieel Dagblad, January 1, 2023.

46 Hoatson, D.M., Subhash, J., and Jaqyes, A.L., 2006. Nickel sulphide deposits in Australia, Characteristics, resources and potential, *Ore Geology Reviews*, 29, 177–241, cited by British Geological Survey, 2008.
47 European Commission, 2014. Report on Critical Raw Materials for the EU, Non-Critical Raw Materials Profiles, DG Enterprise and Industry.
48 International Energy Agency, 2022. Global Supply Chains of EV Batteries; Kara, S., 2023. *Cobalt Red: How the Blood of The Congo Powers Our Lives*. St. Martin's Publishing Group, New York.
49 Henckens, T., 2021. *Governance of the World's Mineral Resources. Beyond the Foreseeable Future*, Elsevier, Amsterdam.
50 Dutch Wind Energy Association. Rare earths in wind turbines, Fact sheet.
51 U.S. Geological Survey, Mineral Commodity Summaries, Rare Earths, January 2023.
52 Henckens, 2021. *Governance of the World's Mineral Resources*.
53 "China merges 3 rare earths miners to strengthen dominance of sector," *Financial Times*, December 23, 2012.
54 U.S. Geological Survey, 2022. Rare Earths, Historical Statistics, Data Series 140.
55 Dutch Wind Energy Association. Rare earths in wind turbines, Fact sheet.

6 The circularity of electric cars

Electrification has major implications for the mix of resources that make up the automobile. Eliminating gasoline and diesel from the transport domain can make a significant contribution to preventing further climate change—provided, of course, that the electricity used to manufacture and run electric vehicles is generated sustainably. Gasoline and diesel will disappear from the picture, but other raw materials will replace them: copper and rare earths in the electric motor and cobalt, lithium, nickel and—again—copper in the batteries.

Gasoline or diesel literally go up in smoke. With electric cars, only two direct emission sources remain: tires and brake linings, both due to wear and tear. All other raw materials, from lithium to copper and from iron to glass, can—in theory—be reused again and again. This places very high demands on the recovery of raw materials from scrap cars, which will have to be much better than it is today. In fact, taking cars apart thoroughly at the end of their lives will become just as important as making new ones.

Electric cars contain much more nickel, cobalt, copper, lithium, and rare earth metals than traditional cars with a fossil-fuel engine. These metals are mainly found in the battery pack and the electric motor. The battery pack of an average electric passenger car weighs about 500 kilograms, which has led car manufacturers to search for ways to keep the electric car as light as possible otherwise, while maintaining the same strength. Therefore, an electric car contains more aluminum and plastic and proportionally less steel than a fuel car. Nevertheless, the average electric passenger car is roughly 300 kilograms heavier than a fossil-fuel car.

DOI: 10.4324/9781003509431-6

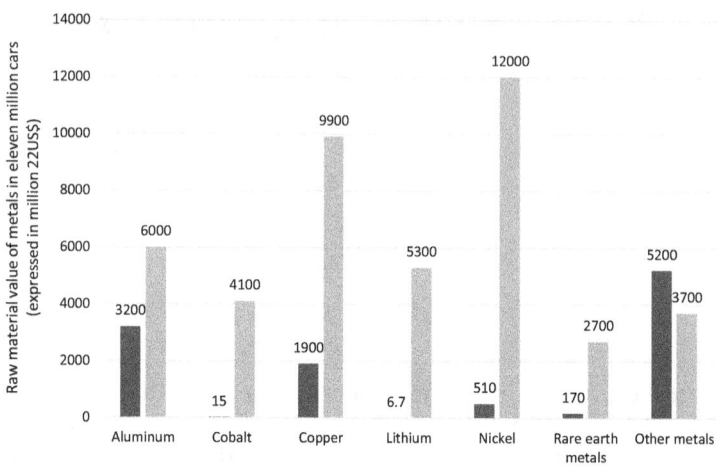

Figure 6.1 Raw material value of the metals in 11 million passenger cars. The left columns refer to fossil-fuel cars; the right columns to electric cars. Roughly 11 million cars were taken off European roads in 2020, and about 60% of these scrapped within the European Union. The raw material value of individual metals is based on their average price between 2000 and 2022, indexed to their value in 2022. For lithium, it is based on the average price between 2010 and 2022. The total raw material value of 11 million fossil-fuel cars is about $11.5 billion ($22) and that of 11 billion electric cars about $44 billion ($22). The "other metals" category consists mainly of steel. The values for electric cars are based on the battery mix estimated by the International Energy Agency for 2040.

Electric cars contain almost no platinum and palladium because the catalytic converter in the exhaust is no longer needed, and the amount of zinc is significantly less in an electric car than in a fossil-fuel car. The raw material value of the metals in an electric car is about four times that of the metals in a fossil-fuel car: in 2022, this was about €4,000 in an average electric car versus about €1,000 in an average fossil-fuel car (see Figure 6.1). Note that batteries represent 30–40% of the purchase cost of an electric car.[1] The raw material value on which Figure 6.1 is based on data from the US Geological Survey.[2] The prices paid for the metal fractions produced by car shredding companies are, however, lower, because they are "contaminated" mixtures of different metals, which limits their uses.

The circularity of electric cars 105

This particularly concerns iron, aluminum, and copper fractions, and not lithium, nickel, and cobalt, as the batteries containing these metals are removed from the vehicles before they go to the shredding company.

> Michel Noordam and his wife Natasja proudly showed us (Martijn Boelhouwer of Auto Recycling Nederland and Theo Henckens) around their car dismantling company in Driebergen-Zeist in the Netherlands, which processes an average of four cars a day. They showed us how, as a first step, all fluids are extracted from the scrap car. These include fuel, motor oil, brake oil, windshield wiper fluid, coolant, fluid from hydraulic systems, and fluid from the air conditioning system. After the oil filters, fuel tanks, batteries, and tires have been removed, the car is ready for further dismantling. How many and which parts are removed from the car and the method of storage of the cars at the site depends, among other things, on the car's age. Young damaged cars are photographed and go to the "car hotel," where they are stored dry and separately. Disassembly of these cars takes place according to the demand for the parts. This can be anything, from doors to engine blocks, car seats, mirrors, and exhausts. These are often removed quickly because, after all, these are relatively new parts. After a while, these "new" cars are moved to an uncovered part of the yard. After any further dismantling, they are stacked together with older cars, ready for removal to the car shredding plant.
>
> The Noordam family's company has an automated parts storage facility, where many thousands of parts are stored in an orderly fashion and can be found again in no time. Not only parts suitable for reuse are dismantled, but also parts that are valuable due to the price of raw materials, such as catalytic converters, alloy wheels, and aluminum and copper components. The extent to which this is done is based on an estimate of how much a part will sell for versus the time it takes to disassemble and store it.
>
> Natasja explains that they dismantle very few electric cars, mostly because it is unclear what condition the traction batteries of damaged electric cars are in. If the battery is fully intact, the value is high, perhaps over €10,000. However, this

> can only be established after proper examination by a specialist. A solution to this problem could be for all batteries to be inspected by a certified company after dismantling and for the insurance company (or the person who delivers the car) to receive compensation based on this. Such an inspection report would also safeguard the car dismantling company from claims for non-functioning or unstable batteries. Certified companies for the inspection of car batteries do not yet exist in the Netherlands. However, once the European Union's new Batteries Regulation comes into force, a system of inspection of used batteries and certification of inspection companies seems necessary.

As far as the transition from fossil to electric is concerned, what is particularly striking in Figure 6.1 is the huge increase in the value share of aluminum, cobalt, copper, lithium, nickel, and rare earth metals. Nickel alone could represent more than a quarter of the raw material value of metals in electric cars following the transition from fossil to electric (this assumes the battery mix estimated by the International Energy Agency for 2040). Nevertheless, the use of nickel and cobalt in car batteries is expected to decline, and these metals will gradually be replaced by other metals that are less problematic. But for the next decade, the raw material value distribution will be as shown in Figure 6.1. The raw material value of the "other metals" in electric cars is lower than in fossil-fuel cars. This is mainly because of the elimination of the platinum group metals, because less zinc is used in electric cars, and because steel is increasingly being replaced by aluminum and plastics.

If market prices of copper, cobalt, lithium, nickel, and rare earth metals rise due to increasing demand as a result of the transition from fossil to electric, it is not inconceivable that the total raw material value of the metals in electric cars will become even higher than indicated in Figure 6.1.

Based on the processing of six million fossil-fuel cars per year, the combined turnover of car recycling companies in the European Union is estimated at about €1 billion per year.[3] Given the higher value of raw materials in electric cars, this could quadruple with the transition from fossil to electric.

The way in which a car is disassembled and further processed is very different for electric cars. An electric car has far fewer fluids: just the windshield wiper fluid, brake oil, and fluids in the hydraulic and air conditioning systems. It therefore has no engine oil, no coolant, and no fuel residue. The electric car is also less complex and contains far fewer parts than a fuel car. In fuel cars, the ferrous metal fraction represents the main value of a scrap car; in the future, it will be the non-ferrous fraction. Five non-ferrous metals (nickel, copper, aluminum, cobalt, and rare earths) represent more than 90% of the raw material value of the metals in an electric car. Nickel and cobalt are mainly in the lithium-ion batteries and rare earths in the electric motors; copper is mainly in the electric motor, battery, and wiring; and aluminum, as now, remains largely in the structural parts of the car, including the battery pack housing.

The auto recycling industry is at the beginning of this development and as yet has no experience with the mass dismantling of electric vehicles. It is essential for the industry to prepare timely and well for this and for governments to create the necessary conditions in which it can take place.

Currently, the average electric car is still more expensive than a fossil-fuel car. However, the difference is decreasing rapidly, not because of a decrease in the cost of raw materials, but mainly due to the increasingly large-scale production of electric cars. This leads to the conclusion that the raw material component will take up a proportionally larger part of the value of the car, especially as the cost of raw materials increases further due to high demand.

There are currently two aspects to car recycling: disassembly and the sale of car parts, and the optimal separation of metal fractions from the remaining scrap metal and their sale. Following the transition from fossil to electric, dismantling will be simpler as electric cars have far fewer parts than fossil-fuel cars. Commercially, the balance will therefore tilt toward the separation of the various metals, as they will represent a proportionately greater value than at present. Car recycling will also be further segmented: in addition to dismantling and shredding companies, there will be separate companies for testing and processing car batteries and dismantling electric motors. The industry is likely to become more complex with a higher turnover, a more skilled labor force, and a changing output. This requires further professionalization and, above all, scaling up.

In the early 1990s, there were many tens of thousands of car dismantling companies in Europe, with often marginal operations. For a long time, scrap car processing was not well regulated, and serious soil contamination often took place because there were no facilities to properly collect the various liquids. A salvage yard was not something you wanted to have next door.

On September 18, 2000, the European End-of-Life Vehicle Directive came into force. This obliges the Member States of the European Union to better regulate the processing of end-of-life vehicles. The main purpose of the Directive is to prevent environmental pollution and to ensure that as few end-of-life vehicles as possible end up in landfills or are abandoned.

The End-of-Life Vehicle Directive centers on producer responsibility. Car manufacturers and car importers are responsible for ensuring that cars are disposed of in an orderly fashion at the end of their lives and that at least 95% by weight is reused or otherwise put to good use, of which at least 85% must be reused. These percentages apply as of 2015.

With the introduction of the End-of-Life Vehicle Directive, EU citizens can take their end-of-life vehicles to a treatment facility free of charge. End-of-life vehicles must then be processed in such a way that as much of the materials as possible are reused, recycled, or otherwise given a useful purpose, for example through energy recovery. From January 1, 2015, a maximum of 5% of the average vehicle weight may still end up in landfill. The Directive is quantitative rather than qualitative, the idea being that the more kilograms are reused in any acceptable way, the better, even if this is in low-value applications.

With the exception of aluminum and iron, only a small proportion of the metals in scrap cars are currently functionally recycled:[4] these are platinum and, to a small extent, cobalt, gold, manganese, molybdenum, palladium, rhodium, and silver. Most metals end up, nonfunctionally, in other metals or are not recycled at all. Further sorting of the ferrous metal fraction into various sub-categories based on the contents of chromium, nickel, manganese, and molybdenum could make these subfractions more usable in the manufacture of various types of steel for new cars, thus making them more valuable and contributing to circularity.[5] In this way, more than 90% of manganese, chromium, nickel, and molybdenum could be functionally recycled, whereas now more than 90% of these metals are lost as a result of "downcycling."

The End-of-Life Vehicle Directive has resulted in a huge improvement for the environment. Anyone traveling around the United States or in developing countries can clearly see the difference with Europe. However, the flip side is that many of the raw materials in cars are not functionally recovered. Functional recovery of a material results in a product that is directly or indirectly usable without further refining and can therefore be used instead of a virgin raw material or an alloy of virgin raw materials. End-of-life vehicle recycling currently yields primarily an iron fraction mixed with a mishmash of other metals, such as nickel, chromium, manganese, copper, and zinc. This iron fraction is sold to steel-making companies. A second, smaller, metal fraction is the non-ferrous metal fraction, the main component of which is aluminum. This fraction is separated into several subfractions, including an aluminum-rich fraction, a copper-rich fraction, and a zinc-rich fraction. Platinum and palladium are removed separately (from the catalyst), as is lead from the classic lead battery. The other metals in cars are not separated but are part of the ferrous or non-ferrous fraction or end up in the automotive shredder residue. The current End-of-Life Vehicle Directive has no rules on the minimum recovery of separate metals, plastics, tires, and glass.

The average age of a scrap car in the different EU Member States varies between 15 and 22 years. In 2021, there were about 14,000 Authorized Treatment Facilities (ATFs) in the European Union, dismantling an average of about 500 scrap cars per year; that is, roughly 2.5 cars per ATF per working day. Furthermore, there are about 350 car shredders in the European Union.[6]

In the Netherlands, you pay a disposal fee when you buy a new car. In 2023, this was €22.50 per vehicle. This is passed on to Auto Recycling Nederland (ARN), which pays companies involved in the dismantling and processing of scrap cars. These companies must be licensed and therefore meet minimum quality requirements. Moreover, they are not allowed to pass on any costs to the consumer. The car owner can therefore send a scrap car free of charge to an ATF. This system ensures that cars that are no longer usable are not left in the environment. Incidentally, the amounts passed on by ARN to the processing companies are relatively low compared to the other revenues of car processing companies. Used car parts were worth an average of about €130 per scrap car in 2015, and the revenue from the shredded fractions—mainly ferrous and non-ferrous metals—about €285 per ton.[7] Converted into 2022 prices, a scrap car is therefore worth about €400. Incidentally, market prices for ferrous and non-ferrous scrap metal fluctuate quite a bit and can go up or down by a factor of two from one year to the next. In a period of low prices, this can lead to buffer stocks waiting for better times. In fact, the disposal fee is mainly intended to dispose of the fractions of a processed car with a negative value in an environmentally friendly way. This particularly concerns the various fluids, the tires and other rubber parts, the battery, the glass, and the plastic fraction.

The weight composition of scrap cars in 2015 was as follows:[8]

- Plastics: 15%
- Ferrous metal fraction: 70%
- Non-ferrous metal fraction: 4%
- Glass: 3%
- Tires: 3%
- Other (liquids, battery, paint, catalyst): 5%

The ferrous fraction consists of iron/steel alloys. This is mainly steel with small amounts of carbon (average approximately 2%), chromium (average approximately 0.8%), nickel (average approximately 0.3%), molybdenum (average approximately 0.03%), manganese (average approximately 0.7%), and very small amounts of other metals. The ferrous parts of a car are often coated with zinc to protect from corrosion, so zinc also ends up partly in the ferrous fraction.

The non-ferrous metal fraction consists mainly of aluminum alloys (about 80%), copper and brass (a copper-zinc alloy) (15%), and a small amount of non-metals (5%). The aluminum alloys are diverse and, besides aluminum, contain small amounts (0.5%–5%) of magnesium, copper, and zinc.[9]

The composition of passenger cars has changed significantly in the last 50 years, with a marked weight shift from steel to aluminum and plastics. Electric cars contain relatively more non-ferrous metals, in particular copper, nickel, cobalt, lithium, manganese, and rare earth metals, mainly in the battery and electric motor (see Figure 6.2).

In the Netherlands, about 25% by weight of end-of-life vehicles were reused in 2016, in the form of used parts,[10] which is quite a lot compared to many other countries in the European Union. The reuse of car parts is less than 10% by weight in half of the countries of the European Union. A recent study by the French Agency for Ecological Transition (ADEME)[11] gives the following reuse rates for fossil-fuel

The circularity of electric cars 111

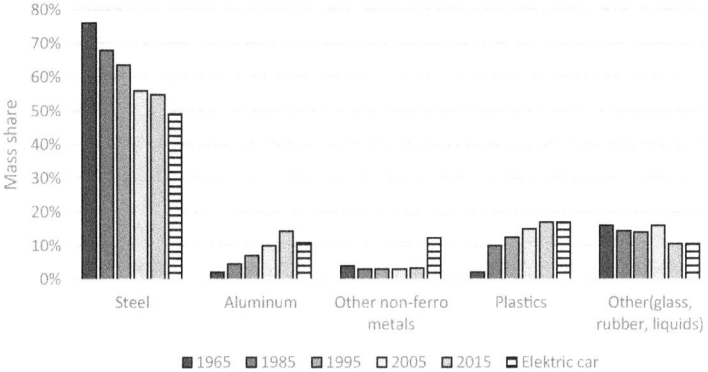

Figure 6.2 Development of the weight share of various components in a passenger car between 1965 and 2015.

car parts in France: plastic parts, 7%; metal-containing parts, 9%; catalytic converters, 20%; tires, 35%; and batteries, 20%.

The End-of-Life Vehicle Directive requires automobile manufacturers to facilitate the identification of car parts. In response, the automotive industry has set up the International Dismantling Information System (IDIS). However, processors of scrap cars complain of the lack of transparency in the system.[12]

Glass, plastics, and copper are not usually separated at vehicle dismantling facilities because selective disposal of these materials is too expensive (i.e., labor intensive) compared to their yields, whereas separate removal of these materials from the shredded material results in a similar yield.

Copper is a special case, being an undesirable metal for steel producers and aluminum smelters because the properties of steel and aluminum are negatively affected by the presence of too much copper. Therefore, processors of scrap cars try to separate copper and brass as much as possible from the ferrous and non-ferrous metal fractions. The main goal is therefore not to recycle the copper, but to guarantee or increase the quality—and thus the price—of the iron and aluminum fractions. The positive side effect is that this results in a copper-rich fraction. Of the 20 kilograms of copper in an average fossil-fuel car, most ends up in the non-ferrous fraction. From there, it can be separated out because copper and brass have a significantly higher specific gravity than aluminum and magnesium. About 20% of the copper remains in the iron and aluminum fractions and is therefore downcycled. As they contain five times more copper per car, the processing of copper from electric cars will undoubtedly receive more attention.

The increasing number of electrical and electronic components may lead to their greater removal from the car at the pre-shredder stage. This may also be the case for electric motors, which contain proportionately high amounts of copper and rare earths. The higher the degree of disassembly of a scrap car before it goes into the shredder, the more selective (and thus better from a raw material point of view) is the recycling of the raw materials.

After dismantling, the car wreck—which then consists mainly of plastics, glass, and metals—goes to a car shredding company. In the car shredder, the wreck is chopped into small chips and then separated into three main fractions: the ferrous metal fraction, the non-ferrous metal fraction, and the automotive shredder residue. The non-ferrous fraction is further separated into an aluminum-rich fraction, a copper-rich fraction, and a zinc-rich fraction, mainly based on the weight and magnetic properties of the shredded material. The metal-rich fractions go to metal smelters, and the residue goes to a post-shredder technology facility, where it is further separated into three main fractions: minerals, plastics, and fibers. Metal is again separated from each of these and sorted into an aluminum fraction, a copper fraction, and a steel fraction. After the separation of the metals, the remaining fraction consists mainly of plastics, textiles, foam, rubber, and cellulose (50–75%) and a heavier (mineral) fraction consisting of powder and dust: mainly glass, sand, paint, and metal (25–50%).[13] This residue can be further separated, with different applications per end product. Ultimately, only a small portion of the shredder residue goes to landfill. The degree of selectivity of dismantling and material separation after shredding is mainly determined by economic considerations, as well as the environmental permit. After all, the companies involved cannot be expected to separate beyond what they are obliged to do and what makes economic sense.

Table 6.1 provides an overview of the current recovery rates of the metals relevant to this book from end-of-life products. Note that these percentages do not apply specifically to automobiles.

As Table 6.1 shows, three of the eight metals in the table (boron, lithium, and rare earth metals) are not yet recovered or recovered

Table 6.1 Literature data on recovery rates of metals from waste products

	Geologically scarce raw material	Critical raw material for the EU	Current global recovery rate from end-of-life products[a]	Economically feasible recovery rate[b]
Antimony	X	X	20%	1%–10%
Boron	X	X	0%	<1%
Cobalt		X	30%[c]	>50%
Copper	X	X	45%	>50%
Lithium		X	0%	<1%
Molybdenum	X		20%	25%–50%
Nickel	X	X	57%	>50%
Rare earth metals		X	0%	<1%

Notes:
[a] Henckens, T., 2021. *The World's Mineral Resources. Beyond the Foreseeable Future*. Elsevier, Amsterdam.
[b] Graedel, T.E., Allwood, J., Birat, J.P., Buchert, M., Hagelüken, C., Reck, B.K., Sibley, S.F., and Sonnemann G. 2011. What do we know about metal recycling rates, *Journal of Industrial Ecology*, DOI 10.1111/j1530-9290.2011.00342.x
[c] Matos, C.T., Ciacci, L., Godoy, León, M.F., Lundhaug, M., Dewulf, J., Müller, D.B., Georgitzikis, K., Wittmer, D., and Mathieux, F. 2020. Material System Analysis of five battery related raw materials: cobalt, lithium, manganese, natural graphite, nickel. Publication Office of the European Union, Luxembourg. ISBN 978-92-76-16411-1, doi:10.2760/519827, JRC119950.

very little. Thus, these metals are almost entirely lost after use. The recovery rates of antimony, cobalt, copper, molybdenum, and nickel are better, but not yet very high.

Boron, molybdenum, and nickel are used in car manufacturing to harden steel, while nickel is also used in traction batteries. Boron and molybdenum are therefore mostly found in the ferrous fraction, with boron limited to about 50 grams per car and molybdenum to about 300–400 grams per car. This makes their recovery complex, especially since the steel in the car contains—in addition to boron and molybdenum—other metals to give it the right properties, such as chromium and nickel. It is therefore technically possible but costly to recover the separate metals from the various types of stainless steel. The most realistic option to functionally use as many of the separate components in steel as possible is to separate different grades of steel and reuse them in a similar application. Nickel is already reused in this way, but this does not yet apply to molybdenum, chromium, and boron.

> *It seems so simple. All we have to do is increase the recovery of metals from waste products, and the extraction of metals from the Earth's crust can be correspondingly reduced. However, things are of course not so simple. If recycling a metal is cheaper than mining it, there is no problem, but if a kilogram of recycled metal costs more than a kilogram of the same metal from a mine, recycling will only take place if it is subsidized. One way to force recycling is for governments to oblige producers, for example of batteries, to recycle a certain percentage of the metals used in the battery. This will in fact be the case under the EU Batteries Regulation and will result in battery producers factoring recycling costs into the price of the battery.*
>
> *The recycling potential of a metal from an end-of-life product depends on the following factors:*[14]
>
> + Concentration: *the higher the concentration, the higher the recycling potential. As a general rule, the concentration should be at least as high as the minimum profitable concentration in ore occurrences.*

- Material composition: alloys, composites, and laminates of different materials make it difficult to isolate the monomaterials.
- Product composition: the more complex the composition of a product, the lower the recycling potential of each of the separate metals in the product (e.g., a cell phone).
- Dispersed use: this inhibits the recoverability of materials (e.g., paint).

The removal of a relatively small amount of different metals from a large amount of a complex metal mixture can be compared to separately removing the spices from soup or separating a baked bread into its constituent elements (flour, milk, yeast, salt). In other words, almost impossible.

Dismantling a scrapped electric car will be different from dismantling a fossil-fuel car, because in addition to the fluids, tires, used parts for resale, and easily removable aluminum parts, the traction batteries, electric motor, and perhaps the wiring harnesses[i] with the copper wiring will need to be dismantled before the wreck goes to the shredder.

Traction batteries are a fire hazard because of the electrolyte contained in them, and therefore require expert disassembly. Traction batteries in vehicle dismantling facilities can be divided into three categories: batteries from cars that have been in an accident, batteries from cars at the end of their life—currently mainly hybrid cars—or batteries with factory defects. The first step is to examine whether the batteries are still usable in other applications. Usually, they still have at least 80% of their original capacity, which means that they can be used for stationary energy storage, for example. Another possibility is to restore the battery to its original capacity by replenishing the lost components in the cathode. However, quality guarantees for the second life of these batteries are then required.

---

i A wiring harness is an assembly of electrical cables or wires that transmit electrical current or signals (Wikipedia).

116 The circularity of electric cars

Battery recycling can be done in two ways. The first is to disassemble the most valuable components of the battery (such as the cathode and anode) and reuse them to produce new batteries. This is called "direct recycling." Direct recycling requires a relatively large amount of manual labor, except when batteries are so uniform that disassembly can be automated. While this will certainly become an important option once large numbers of end-of-life batteries become available, this will not be before 2040. Direct recycling involves regenerating the cathode by restoring the lithium content to its original level. It is especially useful for LFP batteries, whose cathode always contains the same weight ratio of cathode materials, unlike batteries containing nickel and cobalt, the cathodes of which have varying weight ratios.

The second recycling method is much cruder. The battery is shredded, then the most valuable metals separated through a combination of thermal, chemical, and mechanical processes. Technically, each metal can be separated from the shredded material to a high degree of purity, but high costs mean that recycling is currently limited to the most valuable metals, such as nickel, cobalt, copper, and aluminum. Lithium is not currently recycled because it would produce lithium that is more expensive than virgin lithium from a lithium mine. Again, this will change in the future as the EU Battery Regulation requires battery producers to ensure a minimum recovery rate of various metals from batteries.

On the Auto Recycling Nederland website, Martijn Pronk, owner and founder of Used Car Parts, talks about his vehicle dismantling company. Parts that can still be used are cleaned to look like new, then photographed and packed in a resealable bag. The contents are described in detail and advertised on the internet. Every day, DHL comes to pick up the sold packages. His company looks more like a mail order company than a vehicle dismantling facility, says Martijn. I decide to try it out: I enter the make and model of my car and find over 85 different parts in stock. Martijn explains that the more plastic, glass, and rubber are removed from the scrap car, the more the shredding company will pay for it, because there are relatively more metals in the stripped car, which shredding companies like to see.

The new EU Battery Regulation, on which a preliminary political agreement was reached in December 2022 between the European Commission, European Parliament, and European Council, is a proposal to improve the sustainability and circularity of batteries. The agreement includes mandatory requirements for battery sustainability, such as minimum collection rates, minimum recycling efficiencies, minimum recovery rates of certain critical metals, and minimum proportions of recycled metals in new batteries. Minimum collection targets are set of 45% in 2023, 63% in 2027, and 73% in 2030 for portable batteries, and 51% in 2028 and 61% in 2031 for LMT batteries (light means of transport batteries, such as in e-bikes). The minimum recycling efficiency for EV batteries will be 65% as of December 31, 2025, and 70% as of December 31, 2030. The minimum recovery of metals from recycled batteries is shown in Table 6.2. Note that these sustainability requirements will be considered the manufacturer's responsibility, and the EU Battery Regulation will be directly binding.

The recycling of car batteries is still in its infancy as there is still little supply. However, the new EU Battery Regulation makes the question whether battery recycling will become profitable in the future irrelevant, as producers will be obliged to ensure minimum recovery rates of the most important metals. Battery producers will therefore automatically consider the costs and revenues of recycling waste batteries when pricing new batteries.

Battery recycling must be customized because of the wide variety of battery compositions, and this is likely to remain the case for decades to come as battery innovations are constantly taking place. It is therefore conceivable that battery producers will take back the

Table 6.2 Requirements for minimum metal recovery from recycled batteries in the new EU Batteries Regulation

	Minimum recovery as of Dec. 31, 2027	*Minimum recovery as of Dec. 31, 2031*
Cobalt	90%	95%
Copper	90%	95%
Lead	90%	95%
Lithium	50%	80%
Nickel	90%	95%

118 The circularity of electric cars

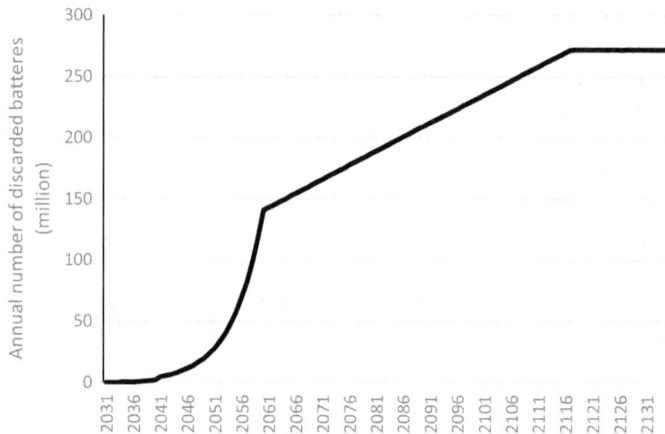

Figure 6.3 Indicative estimate of the number of discarded car batteries between 2031 and 2131. This assumes that the number of electric cars increases exponentially until there are only electric cars on the road in 2060. At this point, the increase in the number of discarded electric batteries changes from exponential to linear. I assume that a situation is reached where automobility in the world is equal to that in the European Union today—if at least the fair scenario is followed—in around 2120, and that the world population is no longer increasing at that time. At this point, the number of batteries discarded annually stabilizes.

batteries that they have produced in the future and integrate them into the battery production process, instead of using external recycling companies to recycle the batteries.

The number of discarded batteries will increase exponentially until the sale of new fuel cars has stopped and all new cars are electric. The increase will then become linear, stabilizing after market saturation around 2120 in the fair scenario. See Figure 6.3.

> Director Paul Dietz of Auto Recycling Nederland told me in an interview on March 27, 2023, that he expects the reuse of discarded EV batteries in a second application to remain limited, at least for now, mainly because of the rapidly improving reliability and energy density of new batteries (i.e.,

> more capacity in a smaller casing) coupled with ever-lower prices. This means that people are likely to prefer a new battery for the time being.

While the infrastructure for recycling lithium-ion batteries from electric cars is virtually non-existent, that for portable lithium-ion batteries—rechargeable and non-rechargeable—is more developed, as smaller lithium-ion batteries have been in circulation for some time. In 2021, two-thirds of lithium-ion battery recycling took place in China and about 20% in Europe.[15] It is notable that China stood head and shoulders above all other countries in terms of the number of publications on lithium-ion recycling and the number of patents granted related to lithium-ion recycling in the 2010–21 period.

The amount of copper and rare earths in electric motors makes it interesting to remove them from electric cars before the car goes to the shredder. Rare earths are found mainly in the magnets of the electric motors and in nickel metal hydride batteries in hybrid cars (there are almost no rare earths in lithium-ion batteries). Rare earths are also used in small quantities in printed circuit boards. Technically, therefore, it does not seem to be too complicated to remove rare earths in decent percentages from end-of-life cars.

> **The mystery of the missing cars**
>
> *Over 30% of old cars in the EU disappear off the radar. They are not registered as being processed by an authorized end-of-life treatment facility, nor are they registered as being exported. In 2017, about 11 million vehicles under 3.5 tons were removed from national vehicle registration systems in the European Union. Of these, about 6.5 million were formally reported as end-of-life vehicles and about one million as exported from the European Union. This means that about 3.5 million vehicles disappeared off the EU radar in 2017.[16] The main reasons are presumably: export to EU Member States with poor registration systems, illegal processing, and illegal exports to countries outside the European Union. To this may be added the fact*

that some of the scrap cars processed in authorized treatment facilities are not, or not properly, reported. The illegal processing of scrap cars in the European Union and the illegal export of scrap cars to countries outside the European Union are particular problems, because it is unclear whether the scrap cars are processed properly or perhaps reused as unsafe and polluting vehicles.

Figure 6.4 shows that, in 2017 and 2018, 480,000 vehicles were dismantled in the Netherlands and 390,000 vehicles with Dutch license plates were exported, about 90,000 of those to a country outside the European Union. The number of cars with foreign license plates exported through Dutch ports in the same years was about 260,000, of which about 60,000 to a country outside the European Union. These were largely cars with German license plates. A significant proportion of these

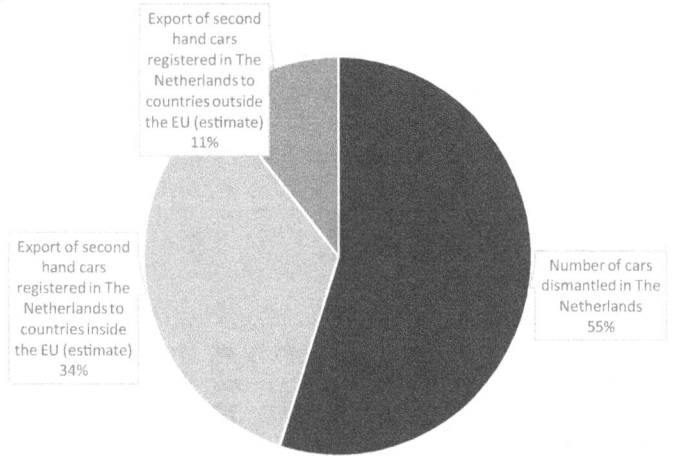

Figure 6.4 Dismantled and exported used cars with Dutch registration certificates in 2017 and 2018. The total number of dismantled plus exported used cars in 2017 and 2018 was about 870,000.

Source: Figures from the Netherlands Environment and Transport Inspectorate, 2020. www.ilent.nl/documenten/rapporten/2020/10/26/rapport--used-vehicles-exported-to-Africa

export cars had as their destination Africa, particularly West and North Africa.[17]

Based on customs data, the Netherlands Human Environment and Transport Inspectorate (ILT) has calculated that the price paid for used vehicles exported to Africa varies between 40 and 70 euro cents per kilogram, so between €500 and €850 for a 1,200-kilogram car. The value of a dismantled car, including the reuse of parts, is around €400, so roughly the same. This is in line with the finding of the ILT, which is that cars shipped from the Port of Rotterdam are comparable in age to the scrap cars sent to Dutch end-of-life treatment facilities.[18] The vast majority of used cars exported to Africa have more than 200,000 kilometers on the clock.

According to European regulations, scrap cars may not be exported to a country outside the European Union, as they are formally considered to be chemical waste because of the toxicity of the fluids they contain. However, used cars can be exported. This means that it is possible that scrap cars are being exported on a large scale as used cars and driven for a while, for example in Africa, before being used as a source of car parts, with one car being cannibalized to run another. End-of-life cars from which potentially polluting substances such as the fuel, other liquids, and the battery have been removed, may be exported to countries outside the European Union, because the end-of-life cars are then no longer chemical waste but "ordinary" waste. Importing countries may of course choose to ban such imports of end-of-life cars.

Most of the used cars shipped from Dutch sea ports do not meet the Euro 4 emissions standard, meaning they are more than 15 years old. Libya, Nigeria, and Ghana are the main destinations for these cars. So many old cars are shipped from the Port of Rotterdam that it is impossible for customs to check whether each car is a scrap or a used car. It is therefore quite conceivable that large numbers of scrap cars are illegally exported outside the European Union in this way. This leads not only to an irresponsible situation in the receiving country but also to the large-scale "leakage" of raw materials from the circular economy of the European Union. Insurance companies could help to improve the

> situation, as they often sell damaged cars to the highest bidder at auction but do not know where the car will be sent. Some African countries have taken steps to limit the import of second-hand vehicles to those that meet at least the Euro 4 emissions standard, some countries around the world have banned used car imports altogether, and others have set age limits.[19]

The European Commission is considering a proposal for a radical revision of the existing End-of-Life Vehicle Directive. It is already clear that this will focus on increasing both the circularity[ii] of metals in the automotive industry and the functional reuse of secondary raw materials, so that they replace primary raw materials from the Earth's crust. A minimum will hopefully be established for both, as the current directive has no provisions for this. As the transport sector is a major consumer of raw materials, it is potentially also a major supplier of secondary raw materials. However, with the exception of iron and aluminum, this is not currently the case. Although almost all end-of-life vehicles are reused or put to good use, these uses are often low-value and non-functional. Most of the critical and scarce metals end up in the iron and aluminum fractions and are thus "lost" in cycles in which they are not or only partially functional.

In my opinion, a provision should be included in the revised End-of-Life Vehicle Directive to prohibit cars that have almost reached the end of their useful life from being exported outside the European Union where, for example in Africa, the adequate treatment of end-of-life vehicles and certainly the recovery of critical metals are still limited. This could be done by setting an age limit for the export of used cars to countries outside the European Union. The export of end-of-life vehicles as waste, for example stripped of liquids, should be banned.

> *The U.S. Inflation Reduction Act (IRA) encourages companies in the United States to recycle batteries from electric vehicles in the United States. The IRA includes a clause stating that battery materials recycled in the United States are considered*

---

ii Circularity is the reuse of raw materials recovered from waste products to produce new, similar products.

> Made in America. This qualifies the production of these secondary materials for subsidies, regardless of the origin of the batteries. It is therefore currently more attractive for US companies to recycle batteries (2023) than for their competitors in the European Union, who receive no subsidies for battery recycling (Nick Carey, Paul Lienert, Victoria Waldersee, Dead EV batteries turn to gold with US incentives, Reuters, July 21, 2023). Currently, the most common practice in Europe is to shred electric car batteries into "black mass" and ship this to China for recycling. As long as the cost of battery recycling in China and the United States is lower than in the European Union, there will be little incentive for EU companies to recycle batteries.

For car recyclers, it is first and foremost important that there is a market for their products. After all, materials will only be properly separated if it is profitable to do so. In a free market, the price of secondary raw materials from end-of-life vehicles must be attractive to the buyer, which means not higher, or preferably lower, than virgin raw materials. There are a few ways to encourage this:

- Make secondary raw materials from end-of-life vehicle processing artificially cheaper, provided they meet certain quality standards. This could be done by subsidizing their production.
- Make it more expensive to import raw materials into the European Union that could also be produced as secondary raw materials in the European Union. This could be done by applying a raw material tax at the EU border.
- Oblige car manufacturers to use a minimum amount of secondary raw materials in new cars, sourced from car recyclers.
- Oblige car manufacturers to take back their products that are at the end of their life in their entirety.
- Oblige car recyclers to ensure a minimum recovery level and reimburse them for the costs (by the taxpayers, the producers, and the consumers), insofar as they exceed the market costs of virgin raw materials.

Important for vehicle recycling in the European Union will be the new European Battery Regulation and the Critical Raw Materials Act, the goal of which is to reduce the dependency of the EU on non-EU countries in terms of critical raw materials as soon as possible.

Notes

1 International Energy Agency, 2022. Global Supply Chains of EV Batteries.
2 USGS, Mineral Commodity Summaries; USGS, Historical Statistics for Mineral and Material Commodities in the United States (data series 140).
3 European Commission, Evaluation of Directive (EC) 2000/53 of 18 September 2000 on end-of-life vehicles, Commission Staff Working Document, March 15, 2021.
4 Andresson, M., Ljunggren Söderman, M., and Sandén, B.A., 2017. Are scarce metals in cars functionally recycled?, *Waste Management*, 60, 407–416.
5 Ohno, H., Matsubae, K., Nakajima, K., Kondo, Y., Nakamura, S., and Nagasaka, T., 2015. Toward the efficient recycling of alloying elements from end-of-life vehicle scrap, *Resource, Conservation and Recycling*, 100, 11–20; Ohno, H., Matsbae, K., Nakajima, K., Kondo, Y., Nakamura, S., Fukushima, Y., and Nagasaka, T., 2017. Optimal recycling of steel scrap and alloying elements: Input output based linear programming method with its application to end-of-life vehicles in Japan, *Environmental Science and Technology*, 51, 13086–13094.
6 European Commission, Evaluation of Directive (EC) 2000/53 of 18 September 2000 on end-of-life vehicles, Commission Staff Working Document, March 15, 2021.
7 ADEME, Terra SA, Deloitte, BIOIS, 2015. Évaluation économique de la filière de traitement des véhicules hors d'usage.
8 ADEME, Monier, V., Salès, K., Lucet, L., and Benhallam, R., 2017. Annual report end-of-life vehicles 2015, France.
9 Margarido, F., Novais Santos, R., Durão, F., Guimarães, C., Nogueira, C.A., Oliveira, P.C., Pedrosa, F., and Goncalves, A.M., 2014. Separation of non-ferrous fractions of shredded end-of-life vehicles for valorizing its alloys, Proceedings of the International Conference on Mining, Material and Metallurgical Engineering, Prague, Czech Republic, August 11–12, 2014, Paper no 7.
10 European Commission, Evaluation of Directive (EC) 2000/53 of 18 September 2000 on end-of-life vehicles, Commission Staff Working Document, March 15, 2021.
11 ADEME, 2020. Rapport Annuel de l'Observatoire des Véhicules Hors d'Usage—Données 2018.
12 European Commission, Evaluation of Directive (EC) 2000/53 of 18 September 2000 on end-of-life vehicles, Commission Staff Working Document, March 15, 2021.

13 Cossu, R. and Lai, T., 2015. Automotive shredder residue (ASR) management, *Waste Management*, 45, 143–151; Passarini, F., Ciacci, L., Santini, A., Vassura, S., and Morselli, L., 2012. Auto shredder residue LC: Implications of ASR composition evolution, *Journal of Cleaner Production*, 23, 28–36.

14 Graedel, T.E. and Erdmann, L. 2012. Will metal scarcity impede routine industrial use? *Material Research Society Bulletin*, 37 (April), 325–331; Worrell, E. and Reuter, M. (eds.), 2014. *Handbook of Recycling - State-of-the-Art for Practitioners, Analysts and Scientists*, Elsevier, Amsterdam.

15 Lithium ion battery recycling—Overview of techniques and trends, *ACS Energy Letters*, 2022, 7, 712–719.

16 European Commission, Evaluation of Directive (EC) 2000/53 of 18 September 2000 on end-of-life vehicles, Commission Staff Working Document, March 15, 2021.

17 Environment and Transport Inspectorate, 2020. www.ilent.nl/documenten/rapporten/2020/10/26/rapport--used-vehicles-exported-to-Africa

18 Environment and Transport Inspectorate, 2020. www.ilent.nl/documenten/rapporten/2020/10/26/rapport--used-vehicles-exported-to-Africa

19 UNEP, 2020. Used vehicles and the Environment, A global overview of used light duty vehicles: flow, scale and regulation.

7 The market in service of fair resource management

Are there enough raw materials available in the Earth's crust to be able to replace seven billion passenger cars every 25 years for an extended period? The answer is no, unless antimony, boron, copper, molybdenum, nickel, and silver are used much more efficiently than at present; that is, if their recycling is greatly increased and they are replaced as much as possible with other raw materials that are less scarce. Of course, the answer to the question also depends on the time horizon, as nothing lasts forever. By "an extended period," I mean several centuries.

The second question addressed in this book is whether it will be possible to produce the additional resources needed for vehicle electrification quickly enough without delaying the rest of the energy transition. The energy transition should ideally occur within a period of about 30 years, between 2020 and 2050. Again, the answer is no, unless it is possible to continue to achieve high annual production increases for decades for cobalt, copper, lithium, nickel, and the rare earths dysprosium and neodymium. For cobalt, this will need to be over 8% per year, for lithium about 12% per year, for copper and nickel over 6% per year, and for the rare earths dysprosium and neodymium over 8% per year. With the exception of copper, these annual production increases were achieved between 2017 and 2022, but the question is whether that can continue for another 30 years.

The market will respond to scarcity with price increases, with prices going up when the demand for commodities exceeds their supply. The market will also anticipate future scarcity to some extent. For example, London's commodities futures market, the London Metal Exchange, allows metals to be traded up to ten years ahead.

The market in service of fair resource management 127

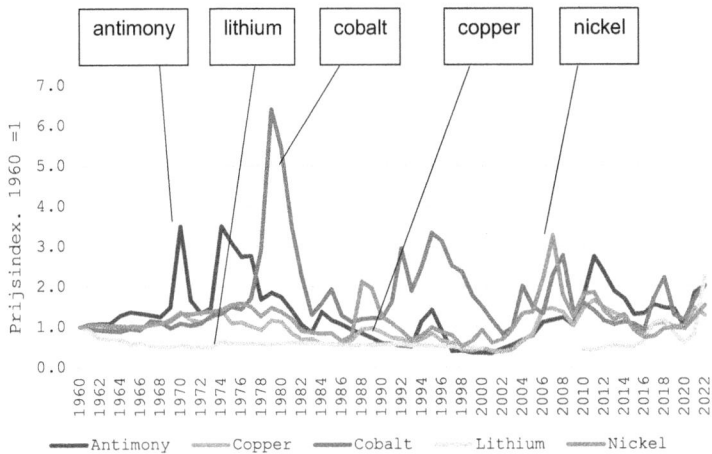

Figure 7.1 Evolution of the price index of five metals since 1960. The figure represents real prices, that is, adjusted for inflation. Annual prices were converted to 2022 prices and then the 1960 price set to 1.

Price data for the commodities antimony, cobalt, copper, lithium, nickel, and rare earths are available from the U.S. Geological Survey (see Figures 7.1 and 7.2). The price index for rare earths is given in a separate figure because the prices of these metals were much more volatile than those of the other five metals. Looking at the two graphs, it is particularly striking that real prices have not changed significantly over the longer term. An effect of longer-term scarcity, or depletion, cannot be detected in the two figures, as no clear upward price trend can be seen. However, there are many shorter-term fluctuations, each with its own background. The large rare earths price increase between 2009 and 2011 was caused by China temporarily restricting rare earth exports during that period, while cobalt price increases in the late 1970s and the 1990s coincided with civil wars in the Democratic Republic of Congo.

As the price trends of the different metals show, the increase in demand for metals needed for electric cars and the rest of the energy transition, which has already been going on for some years, cannot yet be seen. So far, therefore, metal producers are managing to keep up with the sharply increasing demand of 6–12% per year at roughly

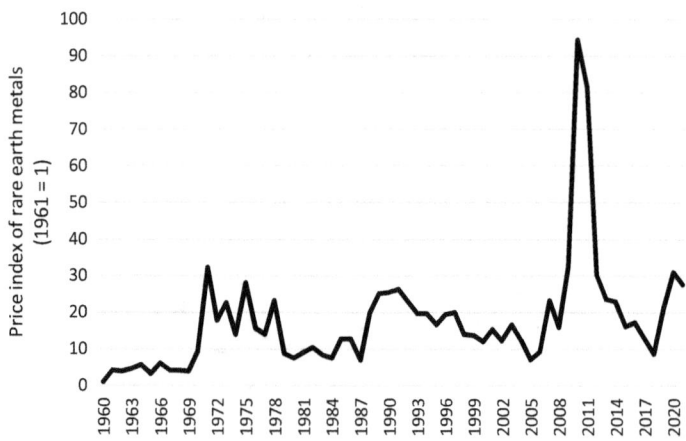

Figure 7.2 Price trend of rare earths, inflation-adjusted.

constant real prices. Metal production is increasingly efficient, despite declining ore concentrations, the greater depth of mines, and the more difficult-to-access locations. However, this is an unstable balance, and a new civil war in DR Congo, for example, could reduce cobalt availability in a very short time. Export-restricting measures by China could also quickly jeopardize the supply of antimony, battery-grade lithium, and rare earths. There is therefore no guarantee that the metals needed for the energy transition will always be available in sufficient quantities: not because of geological depletion but due to wars and other geopolitical tensions.

On February 16, 2023, the Dutch newspaper De Volkskrant *reported that the Swiss-based mining giant Glencore had posted record profits of €16 billion, an increase of 250%. Glencore CEO Gary Nagle attributed this to developments in the global energy market; in other words, rapidly rising energy prices. According to the CEO, the energy transition is contributing to the high demand for raw materials.*

The market in service of fair resource management 129

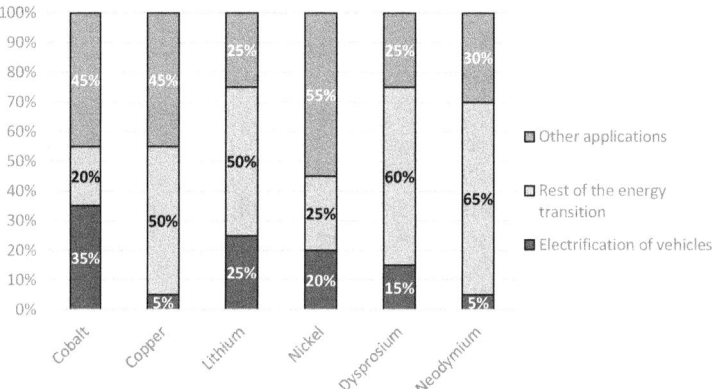

Figure 7.3 Estimated distribution of the application of five metals in 2030. Own calculation, rounded to 5%.

By 2030, a large proportion (45–75%) of the production of cobalt, copper, lithium, nickel, and rare earths will be needed to achieve the energy transition and vehicle electrification (see Figure 7.3). Supply problems will undoubtedly cause countries and companies to compete to maintain their supplies, leading to price increases with negative consequences for the rollout of the energy transition. This will result in the world's dependence on fossil fuels lasting for longer, and in more greenhouse gas emissions, also for longer. Technical measures such as stepping up the recovery of raw materials from products at the end of their useful life are not being realized quickly enough, while the replacement of raw materials with other materials is also a longer-term issue that requires a lot of research. Similarly, conservation measures will not be implemented overnight. Hence, it will take a long time before the required recycling infrastructure of organizations, factories, and machinery has been built and is working properly.

Price increases of raw materials are not necessarily a bad thing. Suppose that the cost of raw materials rises to such an extent that EV batteries become twice as expensive. This is almost certain to influence people's purchasing behavior, and the barrier to buying an electric car will increase, especially if good public transport is available. In this case, sufficient raw materials will remain available for application in wind turbines, power grids, and stationary batteries, although at a higher price. The market can therefore ensure that these applications are prioritized over the purchase of electric vehicles.

It is up to governments to dampen the increase in inequality between the poorer and richer segments of the population. As commodity prices rise, this can be done through tax measures, for example to discourage the purchase of electric sports utility vehicles (SUVs), possibly combined with subsidies for smaller electric cars. It can also be done through subsidies for the construction of wind turbines, battery storage systems, and solar panels.

Fortunately, we know what the most vulnerable commodities are in the energy transition. Countries and companies can, therefore, take preventive measures, for example by building buffer stocks and spreading supplies over several production countries. Companies can also move to build factories in the countries in which crucial raw materials are produced, and some countries may even oblige companies to do so. Examples of this are Indonesia for nickel processing and Chile for lithium processing. China has also long had a policy of promoting the processing of raw materials into semi-finished or finished products in China.

The European Commission is also growing concerned about the availability of metals for the energy transition. In the spring of 2020, the Commission presented a new industrial strategy to help ensure a smooth transition to a green and digital economy. In the fall of the same year, it presented an action plan for raw materials and the European Raw Material Alliance (ERMA) was established to bring together governments, companies, investors, and research organizations. On September 14, 2022, EU President Ursula von der Leyen announced the creation of a European Raw Materials Act in her State of the Union 2022, with the goal of reducing Member States' dependence on non-EU countries for critical raw materials. This announcement was followed by the European Commission's proposal to the European Parliament and the European Council on March 16, 2023, with a draft regulation regarding critical raw materials.[1] At the end of 2022, the European Commission reached an agreement with the European Parliament and the European Council of Ministers on a new Battery Regulation, setting minimum collection rates and minimum recovery rates for several critical metals, as well as a requirement that new batteries contain a minimum amount of secondary raw materials. All in all, there is a clear acceleration in European policy aimed at rapidly increasing the European Union's independence from other countries regarding the supply of critical metals. A report by The Hague Center for Strategic Studies[2] concluded that Europe can learn from China in the area of raw material supply:

> In the Netherlands and other Western countries, the industry has been securing supplies independently from governments. Contrastingly, China has been pursuing a long-term strategy largely due to the deep involvement of the government in industrial extraction and production of raw materials. China is employing a wide range of strategies to develop stages of domestic supply chains, to secure access to strategic resources abroad as well as to enhance their grip on complete value chains.

Incidentally, it is striking that declarations, studies, action plans, and reports on raw materials are always about the short term: how can we ensure that the supply of raw materials to the European Union, our country, our sector remains secure? I note that the European raw materials policy focuses on the interests of European citizens and companies and is limited to the short term. In fact, the message from the European Commission is that Europe should be just as selfish and short-sighted as rivals in other parts of the world, or it will miss the boat. The interests of the world's citizens and of future generations seem to play no role in the reports and policies. This behavior is understandable in the current global context because if a government lags behind in securing resources it is failing its citizens. However, while governments talk of the fair global distribution of resources and the interests of future generations, this is not yet translating into actions.

However, for the longer term (50–100 years), the structural geological depletion of certain raw materials is an issue that must be considered. This mainly concerns antimony, boron, copper, molybdenum, nickel, and silver. The other metals that are important for the transition to electric cars (cobalt, lithium, and rare earths) are comparatively more abundantly available in the Earth's crust. The long-term price trend of raw materials (Figures 7.1 and 7.2) shows that the market is not yet taking into account developments that are still so far in the future. However, once the geological depletion of a commodity becomes noticeable, the market will undoubtedly react with price increases and pressure to use the commodity sparingly will increase. The problem is that by then it will probably be too late to take adequate measures. Ensuring that future generations continue to have sufficient resources can therefore not be left to the market alone. If we want to prevent geological depletion, measures must be initiated well before the market responds. There is still time to avoid being too late, as is the case with climate change measures.

> *The market's response to resource scarcity can even lead to perverse consequences for future generations, as the higher price of a metal makes the exploitation of inferior occurrences of that metal profitable, encouraging further depletion. If the world chooses to safeguard the resources in the Earth's crust at least in part for future generations, then the only way to do so is to set restrictions (quotas) on the annual extraction of scarce resources.*

There have long been calls to use resources wisely and sparingly. More than 50 years ago, in 1972, Principle 5 of the *Declaration of the United Nations Conference on the Human Environment* in Stockholm stated that: "The non-renewable resources of the earth must be employed in such a way as to guard against the danger of their future exhaustion." In 2015, the United Nations set Sustainable Development Goal 12.2 to "achieve the sustainable management and efficient use of natural resources" by 2030. The United Nations Environment Programme (UNEP) established the International Resource Panel back in 2007, the purpose of which is to "build and share knowledge needed to improve our use of natural resources." So far, however, the Panel has largely ignored the topic of resource depletion.

There are therefore plenty of good intentions at the global level, but few concrete measures taken so far, at least as far as mineral resources are concerned. In fact, no targeted and effective long-term policy, such as pricing the scarcest raw materials, has yet been implemented anywhere. In the meantime, the battle between large countries and economic regions to secure as many raw materials as possible for themselves has broken out in full force. This will by no means lead to savings and even less to a fairer distribution of raw materials among the countries of the world.

> **The tragedy of the time horizon**
>
> We can't imagine the suffering of the people of the future, so nothing much gets done on their behalf. What we do now creates damage that hits decades later, so we don't charge ourselves for it, and the standard approach has been that future generations will be richer and stronger than us, and they'll find solutions to their problems. But by the time they get here, these problems will have become too big to solve. That's the tragedy of the time horizon, that we don't look more than a few years ahead.
>
> *A quote from Kim Stanley Robinson's haunting book* The Ministry for the Future. *This fictional ministry created by the United Nations is tasked with standing up for the interests of future generations.*

I conduct my exploration of resource availability from the perspective of the fair scenario, in which ten billion people in the future will own as many cars (all electric) as the average European currently. For a good idea of the impact of this scenario on resource availability, I have not taken into account innovations, resource substitution, and improved recycling. My conclusion is that this scenario is not sustainable unless far-reaching measures are taken to reduce the use of the scarcest raw materials.

There are, however, many uncertainties. Perhaps the world population will peak at eight billion instead of ten billion, as suggested in a recent study by German and Scandinavian researchers commissioned by the Club of Rome.[3] It is, however, also possible that the world population will continue to grow to 12 billion. Perhaps innovations will lead to the much lower use of copper in batteries and electric motors, or perhaps the further development of software will lead to the much smarter and more intensive use of cars and public transport, so that the world can get by with far fewer than nearly seven cars for every ten people, without sacrificing the freedom to which we are accustomed in richer parts of the world. Despite all the uncertainties, it is clear that copper, nickel, cobalt, lithium, and rare earths are the metals that may present supply problems in the short term, and that antimony, boron, copper, molybdenum, nickel, and silver will present a structural availability problem in the longer term due to their scarcity in the Earth's crust and the expected increase in their extraction rates.

Resource flows are global, so policies to save resources are likely to be most effective if they are also global, similar to policies to reduce greenhouse gas emissions. Policies should result in technical measures for the more economical use of resources. Such measures include the following:

- Increasing extraction efficiency, that is, extracting more raw material from the same amount of ore. For copper, for example, the extraction efficiency is currently 84%. This means that 16% of the copper in mined ore is not used but remains on site in the tailings.
- Replacing a raw material with another, less scarce raw material. For example, the replacement of copper with aluminum to transport electricity, or the replacement of fire retardants containing antimony with fire retardants without antimony.
- Increasing recovery efficiency, that is, recovering more raw material from the same amount of waste. For example, only about 57% of nickel in nickel-containing waste products is currently recovered and only 45% of copper on a global scale.
- Increasing usage efficiency, that is, using a product more intensively and/or for longer before it wears out. An example is promoting the use of the shared car. After all, private cars are not used for almost 95% of the time.[4]
- Reducing the downcycling of metals, that is, preventing the metal from being "lost" in the cycle of another metal. For example, about 14% of nickel ends up in the steel or copper cycle after recycling, without the specific properties of nickel being used in these cycles.

These measures will allow the mining of metal ores to be reduced while maintaining the service level of the metals at the current level so that we do not have to sacrifice the services provided by the metals.

Resource use is very unevenly distributed around the world. To calculate the amount of additional resources needed for the transition from fuel cars to electric cars, in this book, I have assumed the fair scenario in which all countries in the world eventually become as prosperous as the average EU citizen in 2050. The fair scenario eventually results in nearly seven billion electric vehicles on the road, assuming sufficient resources and extrapolating the current trend of

The market in service of fair resource management   135

increasing car ownership in the world. However, a fair distribution of resources and electric cars will not happen by itself. We cannot rely on the market to sort it out. Market forces are good when it comes to producing efficiently, but the market does not look far ahead and it fails when it comes to distribution. The market has no vision and no conscience.

Private companies can only be expected to make a token contribution when it comes to the fair distribution of resources, as aptly described by Jorgen Randers:[5]

... A corporation working within the brutal constraints of pure capitalism has little to no chance to contribute significantly to the solution of the main challenges of the twenty-first century. Stopping climate change and alleviating poverty are activities that have much lower return on investment than production of most consumer goods and services. Hence the socially good projects won't win in the internal fight for capital in the firm. The competing firm can of course conduct gestures of corporate (social) responsibility to signal its concern about the long-term future. But only to a fairly limited, and costless, extent. If the corporation does too much more, it will not be around long enough to enjoy the fruits of its expensive bragging... To really do good, the large corporation needs the state to invite tender for the socially good projects...

If global agreements between countries do not guide the extraction and distribution of raw materials in a sustainable and fair direction, then it is to be expected that the current wasteful use and unequal distribution of raw materials will continue. At some point, certain raw materials will become geologically scarce, and the cost of these raw materials will become so high that some countries will not be able to reach the European level of prosperity in 2050. It will be even more difficult for subsequent generations. Governments, meaning all of us, will therefore have to adjust. A global resource policy must strive for a distribution of resources that is fair in two ways: a fair distribution between the countries of the world (intragenerational) and a fair distribution between current and future generations (intergenerational).

The technical measures described above will not come about by themselves and will only be implemented if they are profitable, or they are made profitable. Public policy must therefore make it more attractive to use recycled raw materials through policy instruments that may range from soft and non-mandatory to hard and far-reaching. Such instruments may include the following:

(1) Voluntary instruments. These include *guidelines, recommendations,* and *codes of conduct*.[i] However, these are too non-committal to be really effective, because companies subscribe to them, advertise them, and usually don't do much else with them. Among the non-binding instruments is the agreement to add an *eco-label* to a product, indicating the use of scarce raw materials so that consumers can choose between product A with lower resource conservation and product B with higher resource conservation. However, experience shows that customers mainly go for the lowest price. The same goes for *sustainable procurement* agreements by companies, while well-intentioned and sympathetic, they are not mandatory and on balance deliver little. These instruments do not impose any barrier or obligation on producers or consumers.

(2) Legal recovery targets. This is an instrument that intervenes in consumer and business choice. An example is the European Union's new Battery Regulation. Among other things, it states that eight years after the regulation comes into force, the recycled material content in EV batteries must be at least 16% for cobalt, at least 85% for lead, and at least 6% for lithium and nickel. No later than 16 years after the Battery Regulation takes effect, these percentages must be 26% for cobalt, 12% for lithium, and 15% for nickel. Requirements are also placed on minimum recycling percentages of materials from batteries: as of December 31, 2025, the recovery of cobalt, copper, lead, and nickel must be at least

---

[i] Examples include the OECD (Organization for Economic Co-operation and Development) *Guidelines for Multinational Enterprises,* the *Sustainability Framework* of the World Bank's International Finance Corporation, and the International Chamber of Commerce's *Business Charter for Sustainable Development.*

The market in service of fair resource management 137

90%, and that of lithium at least 50%. From December 31, 2031, these must be 95% and 80%, respectively. The European Union is imposing these targets on car manufacturers and importers, which means that an important effect of this approach will be that car manufacturers will better consider the future recovery of raw materials at the design stage, which is currently barely the case. The recovery of raw materials will thus become part of companies' *Extended Producer Responsibility*. The European end-of-life vehicle and battery directives currently in force do contain target requirements on recirculation, but these do not relate to the degree of recovery of the original raw materials.

(3) Financial instruments. An example is *subsidizing the use* of secondary raw materials instead of primary raw materials. The cost of this could be met by simultaneously levying a *tax* on the use of primary scarce raw materials. Such a combination of subsidy and tax can ensure that the price of the secondary raw material is no higher, or even slightly lower, than that of the primary raw material. A global (or regional) *carbon tax* on all consumer products would encourage the reuse of materials from waste products, because recycling a metal generally uses less energy than producing the same metal from ore. However, a carbon tax in this context helps only if fossil fuels are used to produce metals. Another financial instrument is a *tax* on the non-functional use of a resource, for example if a scarce resource is landfilled or used as filler material or road paving.

(4) Prohibition. A next step on the ladder of measures is to *ban the use* of a raw material for certain non-essential uses. In the case of antimony, for example, this is its use in fire retardants, as there are alternatives.

(5) Annual production quotas. A very direct and effective yet far-reaching measure to limit the use of a commodity is to set an *annual production quota*. This can be done in two ways: under the direction of the producing countries or under the auspices of the United Nations. The advantage of a production quota under the direction of the producing countries is that it can be done relatively quickly and without much bureaucracy. An example already exists, namely Organization of the Petroleum Exporting Countries (OPEC), which regularly consults on the price of oil in relation to production. However, OPEC's goal is to generate maximum income for producers and ensure that its members comply with price and quota

agreements. Fair distribution of oil and gas is not envisioned, nor is limiting production for the benefit of future generations. The best way would therefore be to establish a global agreement on limiting the production of selected scarce resources under the auspices of the United Nations. At the core of such a global agreement would be that producing countries would be paid from a commodity fund hosted by the United Nations to limit the mining of their raw material. In return, the unmined resource would become the property of the international community for use by future generations. The quota that is mined should then be distributed fairly among the countries of the world in proportion to their population and at a set price. This system should generate an income for producers comparable to what they would have acquired without the quota system. Ore processing companies would be able to buy up quotas from countries that do not need them, and this buy-back price would probably be higher than that paid by the countries themselves. After all, scarcity will be artificially created by taking some production off the market. Thus, scarcity is translated into a higher consumer price, while poor countries are automatically compensated for this. The advantage is that the market adjusts and the pressure increases to use less of the raw materials covered by the quota system. The unfair situation that certain countries have a lot of raw materials in their soil by chance and other countries are resource-poor is not immediately reversed. However, an increasing amount of a scarce resource in the Earth's crust gradually becomes the property of the international community, with the possibility of subsequently distributing the resource fairly among the countries of the world in the future. Equity with respect to future generations requires cooperation at the global level, without which the law of the jungle prevails, at the cost of developing countries and future generations.

> *In his book* 2052: A Global Forecast for the Next Forty Years, *Jorgen Randers worries about whether democracies and the free market, in their current set-up, are adequate to guide when it comes to the long term and future generations:*
>
> Both democracies and free markets tend to choose that cheaper route. Both are short term. Both are more than

> willing to disregard long-term costs. Both are strongly motivated by immediate savings. As a result wise action tends to be postponed. Action is achieved only after crisis has struck, not in preparation for future shock. It is simpler to reach agreement on the need to build higher levees after the water has broken through than when high water still remains a theoretical possibility.

An artificial increase in the price of scarce raw materials through taxes or charges is effective in achieving savings in the use of those raw materials. This is because the market will then create a depressing effect on sales of products containing the more expensive raw material, and research to replace the more expensive raw material with cheaper alternatives will be promoted. The effect on the automobile industry and individual passenger transport by car is difficult to predict. It may be that cars will become so much more expensive as a result of higher raw material prices that people will abandon their cars and look for other modes of transport. In a country like the Netherlands, people are used to cycling. The electric bicycle may therefore be an alternative for commuting, although the price of an electric bicycle is also expected to rise, as it too has a battery and an electric motor. During the coronavirus epidemic, we also found that much work can be done from home. Another effect could be an increase on the pressure to live in the city rather than the countryside, where people are more dependent on the car. This tails with the policy of constructing new homes as much as possible within the existing urban environment rather than in the countryside and will also inevitably accelerate a further rural exodus. The migration of people from rural to urban areas is a worldwide phenomenon, caused by the increase in scale in agriculture and the lack of other activities that can provide a decent income for rural people. Apart from commuting, people use their private cars for weekly shopping, to take their children to all kinds of clubs, to visit family and friends, and to go on vacation.

> *People do not only buy cars to get from A to B as efficiently as possible. The car is also a status symbol and a showpiece. The powerful sound of a six-cylinder or eight-cylinder*

> engine and the number of seconds in which you can accelerate from standstill to 60 miles per hour has for some (men especially) an almost sexual appeal. The shape, the color, the luxury: these are all aspects based on which the choice is made for a certain type of car, obviously for most people within a certain financial limit. The huge American cars of the 1950s have become collector's items, despite their considerable fuel consumption, while some young people have an apparent preference for fast, black cars, preferably not too big. Show-offs go for cars that cost $200,000 or more, even though they do no more for their mobility than a car that costs five times less. The Toyota Landcruiser and other SUVs provide the air of a tough adventurer or of a mother that puts her children's safety above all else. It's like a Rolex watch: you don't wear it to see what time it is, but to show off and obtain a certain status, at least in your own eyes. These feel-good aspects of the car may partly disappear in the future, and that may not be such a bad thing.

The car gives a great deal of freedom to come and go as you like. While in theory it is possible to do everything you want without a private car, it is undeniable that many people who now own a private car will find it hard to give up the freedom it represents. For most of the world's population, however, owning a private car is still a long way off. If we really want to ensure the availability of sufficient resources for future generations and for people in—currently—poorer countries, then policies that make resources more expensive will be needed to curb the use of virgin resources. As a result, private ownership of cars will eventually become more inaccessible. It seems prudent to anticipate this in good time, which means adapting infrastructure and spatial planning to a future with fewer private cars, more shared cars, more cabs, more rental cars, good public transport, good cycling infrastructure, less freeway expansion, fewer parking spaces in cities, more working from home, and sufficient local facilities. After all, we are already used to having our weekly grocery shop delivered right to our door.

The market in service of fair resource management 141

Dutch and Belgian transport economists on future mobility

Erik Verhoef, professor in spatial economics at VU Amsterdam:

> It is important to focus on stimulating sustainable alternatives, such as cycling and public transport. In addition, we need to invest in smart mobility applications, such as shared cars and smart traffic management systems, to reduce pressure on the road network.

Stef Proost, professor in transport economics at KU Leuven:

> To make passenger transport more sustainable in the future, we need to focus on a combination of measures. Think about stimulating electric driving, introducing smart road pricing, and investing in alternatives such as cycling and public transport. In addition, we need to focus more on reducing travel by encouraging home working and online meetings, for example.

Jos van Ommeren, professor in transport economics at VU Amsterdam:

> To make passenger transport more sustainable in the future, we need to focus more on reducing car use. This can be done, for example, by introducing smart mileage charges, which will make people think more consciously about their travel behavior. In addition, we must invest more in alternatives, such as bicycles and public transport.

Bert van Wee, professor in transport policy at Delft University of Technology:

> To make passenger transport more sustainable in the future, we must focus on reducing dependence on the car. This can be done by encouraging alternatives, such

> as cycling and public transport, and introducing smart mobility applications, such as shared cars and smart traffic management systems. In addition, we need to focus more on an integrated approach to mobility, looking at all forms of transportation and the interactions between them.

The above outlines a future in which things will run their course: rising commodity prices will eventually make private car ownership so expensive that only the happy few can afford it. However, that future may also lead to a drastic efficiency shift with regard to passenger transport that consists, for example, of a mix of self-driving cabs to take people to work, to school, to the restaurant, and to visit family, and private lease cars for longer-term use, such as vacations in other countries. Children can be taken to sports and music clubs by cab robots, and blind people to concerts. The driverless electric cab shows up at the door exactly when you ordered it and drops you off at the requested address, before driving on to the next customer. A driver's license is only required if you want to drive yourself, and medical examinations for the over-75-year-olds will no longer be necessary. The total number of cars can be drastically reduced because private cars stand idly by the side of the road more than 90% of the time. Without parked cars in the streets, cities will look completely different. In the former parking lots, there is enough space to park the self-driving cabs when they are not in use.

In the fair scenario, the number of cars can be reduced from seven billion to 700 million, which is half the number of cars today, while ten billion people have a level of mobility equal to that in prosperous parts of the world now. The future fleet of self-driving cabs will cause far fewer accidents, end up far less frequently in traffic jams, take up far less space, consume far less energy, cost far less, and require far fewer resources than the vehicles currently in use. At the same time, a large new group of users will have as much freedom as current car drivers, without the need to expand highways, at least in the part of the world that is already prosperous.

> *Self-driving cabs are no longer the stuff of science fiction. On August 14, 2023, the news was that San Francisco would allow self-driving cabs in traffic. Experiments had already*

> taken place with robot cabs in a limited part of the city and only in the evening and at night, but those restrictions were now being lifted. Although the decision of the California Public Utilities Commission was reported by the Dutch newspaper De Volkskrant *to be controversial, the business community is behind it. Will drive-in restaurants and drive-in movie theaters still exist in a future of self-driving cabs? And what will happen to out-of-town stores and endless sprawling suburbs with a parking space in front of every house? How will industrial districts along freeways that are difficult to reach by public transport be viewed? Will more space be given to cars or to nature in densely populated countries? The huge increase in the number of cars has left a big mark on the use of public space. In fact, the appearance of any residential neighborhood is largely determined by parked cars. Until now, most municipalities' policy has been that people should be able to park their cars as close to their homes as possible, while the neighborhood is still green and children are able to play safely outside. Apartment complexes are provided with underground parking garages. What will be the impact on future city neighborhoods of a growing number of shared cars and self-driving cabs and a corresponding reduction in individual car ownership? It is certain that mobility will remain a defining factor in future spatial design, while it is still unclear to what extent the dependence of large groups of people on private cars can be reduced.*

There will of course be resistance if, for the sake of saving resources and for the sake of generations to come, private car ownership is made more expensive. Consider the yellow-vests movement in France, which arose in response to plans by the French government to increase taxes on gasoline and diesel. Despite this almost certain opposition, it is prudent to start taking steps to slow the growth of individual automobility and halt the existing growth trend from 1.4 billion fossil-fuel cars today to possibly about four billion electric cars by 2060, rising further to as many as seven billion electric cars upon completion of the fair scenario over a century from now.

> *In his book* Extracted,[6] *Professor Ugo Bardi of the University of Florence aptly compares the approach to the climate and resource crises to the pointless struggle of the Red Queen in Lewis Carrol's famous book* Through the Looking-Glass. *Everyone in the Red Queen's kingdom had to run as fast as they could just to stay in the same place, and Sarah Palin of the Republican Party in the United States seems the perfect personification of the Red Queen with her statement "drill, baby drill" in her call to increase oil extraction in Alaska. In the battle for resources, we are all running faster and faster with the result that they are only being depleted faster. We are heading in the wrong direction.*

One thing is certain: we must move away from the current car culture, in which the automotive industry tends to continue to market heavier, more powerful, faster, and sexier cars, whether fossil or electric. The SUV reigns supreme, but billions of SUVs on the roads and streets are incompatible with responsibility for the climate, for our resource supply, and for future generations.

Notes

1 European Commission, 2023. Proposal for a Regulation of the European Parliament and of the Council establishing a framework for ensuring a secure and sustainable supply of critical raw materials and amending Regulations (EU)168/2013. (EU) 2018/858, 2018/1724 and (EU) 2019/1020, COM(2023)160final 2023/0079(COD), March 16, 2023.
2 Patrahau, I., Singhvi, Rademaker, M., van Maanen, H., Kleijn, R., and van Geuns, L., 2022. Securing critical materials for critical sectors, Policy options for The Netherlands and the European Union, HCSS Geo-Economics, December.
3 *Volkskrant*, March 28, 2023, p. 3.
4 Factcheck: "A car is stationary 95% of the time," https://factory.fhj.nl/factcheck-een-auto-staat-95-procent-van-de-tijd-stil/, January 10, 2018.
5 Randers, J., 2012. *2052: A Global Forecast for the Next Forty Years.* Chelsea Green Publishing, White River Junction, VT.
6 Bardi, U., 2014. *Extracted. How the quest for mineral wealth is plundering the planet. The past, present and future of global mineral depletion.* A report for the Club of Rome. Chelsea Green Publishing, White River Junction, VT. Originally published in 2013 in German with the title "Der Geplünderte Planet" by oekom verlag GmbH, Munich.

Epilogue

By the time car ownership of the average world citizen has reached the same level as that of the average EU citizen today, some essential resources will have been depleted. Can we comfort ourselves with the thought that this will not be until 100 years from now at the earliest and that innovation and the free market will have solved the problem by then? I think not.

It is not just about cars but about material prosperity in general. Upon reaching a level of prosperity in the world equal to that in the European Union in 2050, the resource pie will be over. At least, it will if we continue to use resources in the same wasteful way as we do today. That is the consequence of equality in the world.

People in the more prosperous parts of the world are uncomfortable, as migration from poorer areas of the world continues. Seeking a more decent life for themselves and their children, people are migrating en masse to more affluent areas of the world. Many people in the West feel that their level of prosperity will be difficult to maintain if the flow of migration becomes too massive, never mind the problems associated with cultural differences between newcomers and natives.

The best structural remedy against uncontrolled migration is for all countries in the world to move toward equal prosperity at a reasonable level. Until this happens, migration flows will persist. However, the dilemma is that equal prosperity in the world, for example at the level of prosperity in the countries of the European

Union, risks being accompanied by the depletion of some resources. This tide can only be turned if drastic conservation measures are taken in time. If "growth" continues as it is, each new generation will extract more raw materials from the Earth's crust than all previous generations combined. Clearly, this cannot continue to go well. Technical solutions exist; the task is to implement them quickly. If we wait for the market, we will be too late.

Index

all solid-state batteries (ASSBs) 26–7
anodes: battery 24; production 51
Aperam (company) 85
arguments for the electric car 6
ARN (Auto Recycling Nederland) 109–10
ASSBs (all solid-state batteries) 26–7
assumptions, scenario 6–12
Auto Recycling Nederland (ARN) 109–10

Bardi, Ugo 144
batteries 17–18, 20–8; all solid-state batteries (ASSBs) 26–7; anodes 24; cathodes 23–4; EU Battery Regulation 117; fire safety 26, 115; production 51; recycling 116–19
Biden, Joe 6
BYD (car brand) 5, 51

car ownership data 2–3
cathodes: battery 23–4; production 51
CATL (Contemporary Amperex Technology Co. Ltd) 27, 51
China: Ganfeng Lithium (company) 75–6; Huayou Cobalt (company) 82–4; lithium-ion recycling 119; nickel 87; raw materials 42–3, 131; sales of electric cars 9

cobalt 76–84; applications 78; distribution 80–2; Huayou Cobalt (company) 82–4; price index 127; production 79–81
Contemporary Amperex Technology Co. Ltd (CATL) 51
copper 58–69; countries producing 64; demand 59, 61–2; industry 60–1, 65–9; price index 127; production 60–1, 64–9; properties 60; recycling cars 111–12; supply 62–5
critical metals 44–51, 58–99
Critical Raw Materials Act 29, 43, 99

depletion, metals 36–9

ecological footprint, raw materials extraction 39
economical use of resources 134
Edison, Thomas 1–2
End-of-Life Vehicle Directive 108–9, 111, 122
energy as a resource 16–18
Energy Return on Energy Investment (EREI) 39
ERMA (European Raw Material Alliance) 130
EU Battery Regulation 117
European Raw Material Alliance (ERMA) 130

148 Index

financial instruments, resource management 137
fire safety, batteries 26, 115
Ford, Henry 1–2
Formula 1 cars 13–14
future, distant 37–9, 57, 131–46
future mobility, resource management 141–4

Ganfeng Lithium (company) 75–6
Glencore (company) 77, 82–3, 128
greenhouse gas emissions data 3–4
Greenland, rare earth metals 93–4

historical background 1–3
Huayou Cobalt (company) 82–4

Indonesia, nickel 87–8
Inflation Reduction Act (IRA), recycling cars 122–3

legal recovery targets, resource management 136–7
lithium 69–76; demand 73–4; distribution 74–5; Ganfeng Lithium (company) 75–6; price 72; price index 127; production 70–3, 75–6; SQM (Sociedad Química y Minera) 75–6
lithium-ion recycling 119

Meadows, Dennis 7
metals 18–20, 25–39; *see also* rare earth metals; *individual metals*; cobalt 76–84; copper 58–69; critical metals 44–51, 58–99; depletion 36–9; lithium 69–76; nickel 84–93; prevalence in cars 27–36; prices index 127; production countries 50–1; rare earth metals 93–9; raw material value 104–7; recycling recovery rates 112–15
'missing' cars, recycling cars 119–22
motivation, car ownership 139–40

Netherlands: Auto Recycling Nederland (ARN) 109–10; recycling cars 105–6, 109–11
nickel 84–93; Aperam (company) 85; China 87; companies 89–90; distribution 92–3; Indonesia 87–8; price 89; price index 127; production 87–91
NZE Scenario (net zero emissions) 41–2

Paris Agreement (2015) 5
private companies, resource management 135
production: anodes 51; batteries 51; cathodes 51; cobalt 79–81; copper 60–1, 64–9; electric cars 51; lithium 70–3, 75–6; metals 50–1; nickel 87–91; rare earth metals 94–5
prohibition, resource management 137

quotas, resource management 132, 137–8

Randers, Jorgen 37–8, 135, 138
rare earth metals 93–9; applications 98; Critical Raw Materials Act 99; distribution 95–6; Greenland 93–4; price 97; price trends 127–8; production 94–5; recycling 98–9
raw materials 16–17, 20, 27–9; *see also* recycling cars; China 42–3, 131; Critical Raw Materials Act 29, 43; extraction ecological footprint 39; metals value 104–7; scenarios 36–7, 53–7; sensitivity analysis 53–7; strategic raw materials 42–3, 50
recycling cars 103–24; *see also* raw materials; Auto Recycling Nederland (ARN) 109–10; batteries 116–19; copper 111–12; encouraging recycling 123–4;

End-of-Life Vehicle Directive 108–9, 111, 122; EU Battery Regulation 117; Inflation Reduction Act (IRA) 122–3; metals recovery rates 112–15; metals value 104–7; 'missing' cars 119–22; Netherlands 105–6, 109–11; rare earth metals 98–9; weight composition 110–11
resource management 126–46; economical use of resources 134; financial instruments 137; future mobility 141–4; legal recovery targets 136–7; metals prices index 127; private companies 135; prohibition 137; quotas 132, 137–8; self-driving cars 142–3; time horizon 132–3; voluntary instruments 136
Robinson, Kim Stanley 133

SAIC (car brand) 5
sales of electric cars 9
Sanderson, Henry 73–4
scenarios: assumptions 6–12; NZE Scenario (net zero emissions) 41–2; raw materials 36–7, 53–7
Seba, Tony 6
self-driving cars, resource management 142–3
sensitivity analysis, raw materials 53–7
Sociedad Química y Minera (SQM) 75–6
strategic raw materials 42–3, 50
synthetic CO_2-neutral fuel 5, 14

Tesla 5, 51
time horizon, resource management 132–3

Volkswagen 3, 4–5; VW Group 51
voluntary instruments, resource management 136

For Product Safety Concerns and Information please contact our EU representative GPSR@taylorandfrancis.com
Taylor & Francis Verlag GmbH, Kaufingerstraße 24, 80331 München, Germany

www.ingramcontent.com/pod-product-compliance
Lightning Source LLC
Chambersburg PA
CBHW051749230426
43670CB00012B/2214